Situations, Sings

JACK COLLOM & LYN HEJINIAN

ADVENTURES IN POETRY

Book design by *typeslowly*
Printed in Michigan by Cushing-Malloy, Inc.
on Glatfelter Natures, a recycled paper

Acknowledgments:
Portions of a few of these works have been previously published
in *Sal Mimeo* and the first *Zoland Poetry* annual

Adventures in Poetry titles are distributed to the trade through
Zephyr Press by Consortium Book Sales and Distribution [www.cbsd.com]
& SPD [www.spdbooks.org]

ISBN 978-0-9761612-4-0

9 8 7 6 5 4 3 2 FIRST PRINTING IN 2008

Adventures in Poetry
adventuresinpoetry.com

Contents

Situations, Sings

Questionably

QUESTIONABLY

Is this one you can answer?
Tell me again just where the gall bladder is located?
Isn't writing this on a blank page as cruel as landing a plane?
Is a red dog famous? Isn't anything cruel and nothing callous?
When did you first ask that and when did you first become aware that you
      were doing so?
Does a rope contain glue or how else does it work?
If there were a necessary connection between the will and the moving of a
      billiard ball, wouldn't the results always be the same?
Did you know that the displays of fireflies are pure courtship?
Aren't I right that in the middle of the night someone—consciously or not—
      writing a few words will have joined the caravan of poetry?
Isn't it so that a bluebird sings several warm-up sounds that are "off the scale"
      before it begins its green spring song?
Did you do it?
What do you mean?
Did the weather turn cold because I yearned for it to do so?
Is a connection more than a line in space, where blue and brown fight in the egg?
Does the connection we call love always involve a fight for life?
If you snap your fingers will it rain?
Is *Anna Karenina* just a pack of lies?
Will the goddam cops arrive any second?
Is this religious or diverting?
For example, do you like to shoot pool?
Wouldn't the very notion of the "non-sequitur" be impossible in the timeless
      world of the dead?
Wouldn't the very notion of the "non-sequitur" be impossible in the timeless
      world of the dead?
How dare you! How dare you?
If you put the word "VITAMINS" on your wall, each letter a new color, does it
      encourage a wild lovelife?
What I saw in the air over the Mississippi—bald eagles, male and female
      swooping, ducking, colliding—was that "mating"?
Wasn't it though! (Does this line let the gods in and out?)
Why *wouldn't* the preschoolers love scotchtape, given its zipping sound, its

inability to get out of hand, its capacity to bind whatever they love
together at the very moment they love it?
"Are you dogging my footsteps, Sailor Ben?"
Will the children be any the wiser?
What's the parabola (in months) of dried oatmeal, untouched, on a porcelain
surface?
Who farted?
Can the idea of "gray areas" be carried too far?
Should I turn on the heat?
Will "four" fit in a genuine feeling?
Shouldn't we question the credibility of our dream?
Can we say Kandinsky was derivative as the Sphinx?
Should we agree?
Will you won't you will you won't you will you continue?
Should we turn back now, before we cross the point of no return?
How much does a prospect weigh?
We're improvising here and isn't that suspect?
How slow must a flash of light be to be properly civilized?
Have you an alibi for the time in question?
Why didn't you get salt while you were out?
Are you sure this is the decaf?
What's that gaping hole at my very feet?
Should I worry about the numbness?
Are we still growing? Where? Where?
Have you been busted?
Is a two-headed zebra really a one-headed zebra with an extra head?
Didn't Bill Murray deserve an Oscar for *Groundhog Day* rather than *Lost
in Translation* (if he deserved one at all)?
Call me an exterminator, willya?
What's going on?
Have the charts been published?
Have you left an impression on your bed?
Will you ever learn to turn off the gas when you're finished cooking soup?
Do you even want someone to come up with answers?
Is there closure anywhere within the color orange?
Is this the exit or just the door to the closet?
Do you wanna put all your eggs in one basket? Or not?
What fresh extravagance is this?
Is a mixture really a mixture?

Is this art or some inefficient real thing?
Why did the sun pick just now to blast me?
Aren't you curious?
What do you care?
Will you just answer the question: should I set the oven at 350° or 325°?
Is there something wrong with me?
Shouldn't we ask Steve Benson?
Can't we just go to the Bronx, take a seat, and stare into the night?
How can a body politic tolerate capital punishment?
Does your boss suspect anything?
Is Salsa a good name for the cow?
Does darkness have more fun?
Do you think the old guy is guilty and, if he is, are we/aren't we guilty too?
Don't you think Apollo is just a little bit narcissistic?
What days are good for you?
Which part of "knob" can't you understand?
If you are through with the Rothenberg anthology, could you return it?
Why do certain initials, such as "R.C.," come to stand for so many different
        and prominent things? Euphony or content?
Do you know the song I mean—is it "CC Rider" or "Easy Rider"?
Is "Clark Coolidge" that difficult to pronounce?
Am I on the right track?
What do you think of Tracy McGrady?
Is the form that the rejection of capitalism ultimately will take not communism
        but religious fundamentalism?
Is a butterfly on a mouth too corny for words?
Did I overhear correctly what the elderly neighbor just said ("I'm going out to
        bowl, honey")?
How can the statisticians more perfectly zoom in on blame?
Shouldn't we stop eating tuna?
How would you be different if cave-painting hadn't come along?
I'm sorry, is this your seat?
How do they do it, with no external organs?
The paper behind the poem is generally invisible, but couldn't one think of it
        as having been prepared, in the way that a surface is prepared for a
        painting, for example?
In the photograph in front of me, Daddy walking me along a wintry Western
        Springs street, what was in our minds?
Haven't we seen this movie before?

Mommy, can I have another fruit bat?

Why three books at the same time?

When will I die?

Are you using the pronoun in the singular or plural?

What are tongues for then?

Isn't that all mere speculation?

Do you think toilet paper with jokes or puzzles printed on each square is
a get-rich-quick idea?

Say a woman calls a man "Fuck Face"—aren't there scenarios in which this
comes off as neither angry nor enticing but as calming—neutralizing?

So why not be horrified *all* the time?

Anode odna o agfuoantoa hv noqa roebn?

I see somebody in your eye. Who is it?

Don't all those sharpened colored pencils in the jar make you want to draw
something?

And now, Senator Persiflage, may I come to the matter of your "aunt"?

Is this (*Lyuba asks, pointing to her nose*) Gogol's?

¿Cuánto costa?

Was the crow that dropped the grape in her beak into the lake in order
to mouth off to the idiot who'd accosted her a *typical* crow?

What time is it really?

How long is this going to go on?

Revival

Revival

Winter is not sad, it brings revival of the rocky shade,
Life away from the blaze. Shadows seem, by their shapes, to announce
        constituents
They've drawn to earth, existences they hide or hide within.
One such shadow undulated beneath my rolling cartwheel recently,
A sign of friendship of the sort that always occurs when (in good faith, even if
        it's in a theater) friendliness is expressed,
Though it's hard to combine safety and even the few seconds one needs to
        catch a rhythm
Can bring confusion to the melody, rendering the upward sequence despondent
        or the descending sequence jubilant, profundity ecstatic or surface deep.
Take bluegrass: the very precision of the Scruggs three-fingered banjo style
        triangulates emotions (generally low, etc.) as an engineer does a swamp,
        makes it productive.
Or take poetry: the mere knowledge that there is world "out there" draws one
        from the interior of words, leaving their meanings behind
A burning bush. But then snow is likely; it's a bit like taking a new piece of
        paper, placing
An unrecorded (even perhaps unremembered) moment of one's history in an
        embarrassing context or perhaps a false light
Or even in a bear's womb. If the womb were not shadow it would be tragedy
And we would regard birth as a release from suffering. But once born, one is
        still not safe
Since only the whole, one might almost say "the boring," or at least the slowly
        growing, are safe from light's ravages, which
Leave in their wake "glimmering sparks." We wake, vigilant
But somehow careless of what might occur, inclined to find initiative in
        acquiescence,
Action in pauses, progress in activities we have done no more than observe. Our
        contributions, such as they are, are humbling,
Are wordshadow, are slightly perverse like the beauty a buried "r" brings
To any language, "r" being a round red bear, "r" rolling into every word in which
        it appears so that only the rare foreigner who can articulate it in a
        ridiculous roar

Can wrestle it into the rust of the library, of the temporary library known as
        the strawberry, into the ptarmigan's precise March risk,
Or into any of the other sites which intercept it. "R." I cannot spell it—
        cannot dispel
The flutter, like a montane rill, with which it inches into the "l," and how then
        the two gently subvert
All that rages into beauty. But the waterfall does not exist simply to be
        beautiful;
It brings the water down. Thus gravity is appeased; thus the water trades
        labor for the chance to secretly prepare another evaporation; thus
The cellist bows while her trembling fingers descend the cello's neck and her
        friend struggles for breath.
Likewise, the seasonal statistics in the feet imperceptibly begin their bend
        along a complicated softening
Of the shoe and hardening of the nails in preparation for walking barefoot
Through the azure reflections summer's end unjungles
And autumn's promise muddles, producing dreams—in mine I (one of a
        crew of 5) was sailing away in a portacrib
But the number, 5, of us caused the vessel to become a minor firewheel and
        the golden letters "The Muddled Promise" to blacken
Into ink with which the voyage's botanist made a tiny and intricate but
        entirely abstract drawing, a drawing of nothing.
The point was, it put the fire out. We breathed again, looked about. Nothing
        but blue/blue
Depths were mirrored in the blue/blue heights. The driven plenitude
Reminding me of a waterfall laid on edge, nodding off perhaps, but still
        radiant of its very definition. Soon
—As "soonness"—the waters, having fallen, (will) flow, defining "down"
        —aimlessly
According to strict laws that are nevertheless so tiny dawn throws its hands up
        in surprise
As if declaring independence so as to take its own view of things as they
        dispose themselves constantly along the stream or on its banks anew
Slowly, in such a slowness, in fact, that the generative point in the heart of
        action's initiation is calm, is as calm as a pebble of granite underground
In contrast to which a drop of moisture in a cloud seems wild
As fire. But it's winter. The excitement of cold is like that of marriage, in the
        pressure

That propels the wind that animates the tree that, just as Lin-yi says, in
        achieving nothing achieves everything
At once. The shade alone's worth all the light that borders it, sometimes more
Tree than shadow of tree and at night neither. As for me, I'm in no particular
        hurry
To achieve the general. My split personality only guarantees embrace
Of ambiguity and ambivalence both coming or going through the always-
        open windows that at night admit breezes so cold that as I write this
        I wear a knitted nightcap
Because it's too thick to drink. Oh well, I have the feeling house and land are
        sliding at a good rate
Back from reality, where events come to pass that were long predicted and
        can be regarded in retrospect as having been inevitable, though that's
        not to say that they were *destined* to happen. Or is it
Not vanity to say that Destiny, like Cleopatra, presents a "poop of beaten gold,"
        in contrast to the thick steel plates of inevitability
That reflect the light of the setting sun and bar us from entering
The enlisted mess of "The Golden Vanity" before repetition swallows
        distinctions and substitutes metamorphoses for them? Who
Knows (i.e., who *cares*)? The opaque clouds veiling the sun above seem like
        emblems of the state of
Declare passed through a condition of stage, basically a white seed
Of optimism sprouting in the soil of uncertainty.
But when we bend down to take a closer look there's no gainsaying the
        effervescent *ballgames* going on all around, on a certain scale
Trivial, on another scale epic, and when they are done and history is made
The *scores* will become a decorative system of xylography, numbers crumbling
        away to reveal the numbers at the bottom
Of a page describing trees bent with age, cavorting in a storm, toppled in a
        torrent of emotion
And then slowly rotting but even so partying in phosphorescent death,
        hollowing around
The legible traces of feasting beetles spelling ruin spelling riot spelling
        rejuvenation
And spelling it with three R's, each one darker than the last
Storm cloud before the torrent of rain that swept the air clean, or as clean as
        it can be.
No, winter is not sad; its zigzag revivals cause time's slide to resemble the
        skin of a fish, scales

Riveting. They flash, disappear, appear again differently, the fish robbing the
          rich to give to the poor
Soul whose vast eye(s) like a lunar dish impoverish themselves by means of
          their very and multiple function
Something to look at—something that might reappear in a dream from which
          one wakens trembling
Fellow dreamdwellers and forms a phalanx with which to securely, even
          drunkenly, enter the day
As a time-traveler might, asking "Has anthropology been invented?"
"And if so, by whom?" interposes the round red bear, positing a florid paw
          beside the pale, berry-like nose as if
It bore thorns, like a rose. A poet appears and continues prosaically
To divide things along these lines. He pulls a pear
From a bucket and calls it a paperbagged hallway which he calls a snowball
In turn, but in turning the snowball becomes lightly browned by the light of the
Streetlight at the corner of Russell Street and Benvenue not far from the house
          from which the SLA kidnapped Patty Hearst—remember
How the thought filled the reading room that we are truly prisoners of color
          and form
Our opinions from within the red, green, and turquoise which bar us
And which bear us through the borealis of a cold but brilliant solace
Basking this sixtieth, seventieth winter in which we revive
Life away from the blaze. Sound, of course, becomes
The principle of hope in a waking dream. Pathos binds occurrence to change,
Which means that pathos is at the very bottom of the heap, where substance
          rubs number till the hairs turn.
Beauty cannot be sustained. But whimsy is even more vulnerable,
More flimsy, than beauty, which rides, along with its puff glory, a longish stick
          of duty
That it hopes will transport it into the realm of immutability, the recalcitrant
          horse that was trained by whimsy
To perform a huge, brown contradicting fatness of tiny elements variously
          curved and thereby proceed
From the canyon to the stars. The photograph is silent. There is no trail. The
          rider is picking her way
From a large assortment of ways. In the trail's absence, they gleam like
          phosphorescent arteries. But, after a moment, she sees only one
Heap of boulders, one fern. Riding isn't easy. She has her lunch over her
          shoulder, she's never been on an ocean liner

Named the *Lily Pons* before. With such *games*. She glances over
At something she'd not thought she'd see: the unregulated sea making its plea,
If you can call it that, for eternal nonrepetitive continuation, changing eventually
        into something that is no longer a sea but
A man named George fishing in it one late summer afternoon as tourists flood the
        pier
With gorgeous forked-blob ephemera. George sips his beer, imported Pschorrbräu—
And speaks of beauty—but in speaking of beauty one speaks implicitly also of
        reality and of time.
The rider looks at him from across the stream and sees an alcohol molecule of dream
Autobiography afloat in a greater history about which no one before has been honest
Enough even to make a three-dimensional map, much less
Compose an elegy. Is the possible restricted only to that which has been possible?
Obviously not. But *that's* not "set in stone." And stone itself is like these lines.
Astonishingly similar to members of a family, some of whom were miners, others
        Portuguese
Men O' War. Others were sometimes seen in silhouette, on a distant ridge
Where they might be described as picnickers dining on tiny sausages and pickles in
        the wind
In one of E.A. Robinson's lesser endeavors at glorifying indignity
In bad weather. Infants don't ask to be born, children don't volunteer for the hard
        work of living,
Yet adults seem to have somehow signed up, and wear the white uniform, and face
        east like cows in a blizzard—
Snow driven by winds that are peacefully blasting the landscape. And what, you
        might ask, do we mean by landscape that it's inhabited by cows and blasted
Caregivers? The time scope of any given fishscale of events there shines like a
        microscope falling in a hole.
A big rabbit goes after it followed by a girl, and (philosophically speaking) that's
        writing for you! First there's a microscope, but before that there's both a
        hole and something little, and before that
A gleam in the eye of Uncle Louie. But let's examine what we mean by "rabbit."
        Obviously it's a complex looking for a duplex
In disguise but the television in the next room is distracting, a plot is developing,
        the rabbit is irresistibly drawn
By Sir John T., blowing a trumpet (or did I leap
Once to that conclusion and do I sing now in a minor key, conclusion and key
        linked together like sumo wrestlers

Rolling through a door?), and the flowers seem to illustrate the drawbacks of
universal speech
In a language that is universally incomprehensible and totally unpronounceable
and gets transcribed as #$%&*,
At which E. A. Robinson is shocked. But when we tell him it's a form of
silhouette
He presents a pleasant profile. One of the most penetrating forms of humor
is dramatic humor,
And Robinson, having inadvertently wiped out the family of birds nesting in
his cherry tree, simply added a "g" to his name
Without further explanation. And since every story consists principally of
"further explanation" we must here abandon Robinson-with-a-g to
sing as he likes.
The flowers. The flowers seem to militate against giantism. Not that they're
small—
No more than a single note of music, which, even if it rings for a mere 16th
of a measure,
Fills a little world with radiating sense that, of course, changes as it spreads
Faster than the note-takers can run. Sense outraces pundits to the dance
And by this time the petals, some of them, are plunging toward the ground,
drying
And melting, leaving red and yellow patterns on the ground that only the
melancholy would take as a lesson
In celebration. A rustle; an upward glance; it's a cow, but is it
Sufficiently dramatic, is it milky? It has a perceptible self, a "good nature," but
has it lost its way
Of being "interesting" and at the same moment saintly? This "way" is easier
for plants, and even rocks
Are puzzled by plants, which so eagerly assent and then never come back
Except as something dark and burnable. Constant exchanges of earth and sky
Occur which we can describe but not identify. Rain is battering a field—is
that theater or history or do we yearn in saying so?
Is all our poetry pantomime? Is it more like drumming with little sticks than
like a tiger padding through the
Walnut orchard amid the blossoms raining from the trees? Or is it more like
building with bricks than like a pedestrian crossing an intersection,
The intersection of malleability with itself? As we rise we can look down and
see the little black figures gesticulating, shrinking....

Obedient to rules of friendship they know as if from birth, they spell each other
'S names wrong, but in that wrongness there is such a loving warmth! For
        example,
Panoply calls Key. Key she calls Beloved Bulb. Beloved Bulb (or Key) finds
        Panoply's relentless "warmth"
A little bit like a drink of pure alcohol. What the hell. It's better than a
        mediocre country singer who's been "there" since one was a child
In first grade sitting eagerly, suffused with homesickness, on her chair in the
        "reading circle" waiting for Richard to work his way from Dick to Spot
To whirl of lanky pulp in the dryer. "Remember me!" from a passing truck
Sends the kids into reveries of ice cream from which they're brought back by
        memories of the sharp little niggling ache at the bridge of the nose
        occasioned by the cold
Winter winds that eventually ensued. Meanwhile, two of these walnut orchard
        friends have wandered off
With the cell phone and, worse, the map, whose delicate gray-green and
        lemon-brown filigree indicating altitude and amplitude inscribed in a
        penmanship of extraordinary loveliness
Was even better, ultimately, than its building-with-bricks way of telling one
        where one was, as if
It mattered. The improbability of our being able to forget the door (not to
        mention the name
Of the spring that drives that little thingummy out in order that the door
        might catch
And hold the wind from the floor) made the appearance of the stranger on
        the sofa writing
Uncertainty-theory limericks a shade cinematic until he
Heard his internal editor shout "Cut." He began a sestina whose end words
Were "lights," "camera," "action," "of," "if," and "Eisenstein," but he couldn't
Sleep for the excitement of the dark and oboe stillness, the without that then
        descends the palace steps
Of the throat into the root cellar of the heart. He heard a hexagonal
Repetition of his name whose familiar sound-shape was a mere hallucination—
        he wasn't meant
To be remastered into video and then remaindered on the windy floor. Again
The merry dinosaurs like fawns with heavy hearts performed the rite of spring,
In which the very letters divide and re-form, first to soar, generic flora, fauna,
        then

17

To sink roots and nurture etymologies, binding theories to theaters and ghosts
        to anger and feathers to
The specific flow of a swamp river where two mandarin ducks, breast to breast
Bob in the current as night falls. O fish of the rivers and O frogs, O
        nighthawks and owls, O
Photograph of a harbor scene! The Ark has split into many tiny
Creature-bearing boards abob on the ripples set in motion by the happy fish
        for whom the flood is
A perfect example of envirogenesis. Following out this logic, like a white rat
        climbing a rope
Toward a dark shore, we deduce the inevitability of snows bringing down
        crystal alphabets,
Which in turn bring down "the dark and oboe stillness"
Over this. We spell (and are cast in spells): "raisins; rice; pencils; cheese" and in
        my blue car I go
As if it were everything or at least a blanket over everything. E-v-e-r-y-t-h-i-n-g.
You with the y and I with the g row into the current. I say, "Take care of the
        raisins and potatoes, our sustenance" and you say "Beware of the reasons
Because they love potatoes not wisely but too well,"—but you knew that, know
        that
"They" should not be mistaken for "Troy." Aristotle's horse—but perhaps
        Aristotle had no horse
But only a horse-shaped thought. Socrates *was* a horse, and Plato a horse-
        sandwich
At rest on an ideal platter casting an heroic shadow in a warm (not to mention
        womblike) cave sheltering hungry puppeteers
Who didn't quite understand that they were relevant and irrelevant at the
        same instant in the same "wingspread"
As that which cast the fleeting shadows we call "ourselves." Your name
Slipped under the waves a moment—ahh, there it is! No, only a clump
Of soggy papers oozing ink from letters of an unfamiliar alphabet we take to
        be a code
That flashes wet/dry/wet/dry, etc., as we sidestroke to the rescue. Only a
Cosmonaut could have gone farther or faster. The ever-shifting and always
        self-postponing horizons
Of each letter vibrate concentrically within the horizons of each perpetually
        embryonic word
That rhymes with sky. In a similar way I find myself thinking of dogs just as,
        from the West as the sun is sinking, a cascading bank of fog,

Obviously shaken out of some pure sphere, lands like a cat on the no-man's-
        land
We consistently avoid, refusing even to name it and leaving it to the rats.
        Where we, when we were children, played
At being wild dogs was a platform raised on spindly beech logs above that
        no-man's-land; however
The storks blocked the chimney, we managed to stay warm sipping soup, and
        without burning
Clothes or skin we would rub the spoon, and sometimes even the heated
        rocks, across
Our legs. We learned to run out of fear of beaded wolves, we learned to swim
        out of
Small enclosures and into large. We even observed grama grass growing on
        Schopenhauer's
Pessimism, which he hadn't the will to cut. But now we can laugh at all this
Sky-rhyming and the laughter, for a moment, forms half a ball before it
And a flat surface behind. It's as if the ancient world under its domed
        hemispherical heavens resting on flat Tartarus far below and
        encircled by Okeanos had turned
State's witness for a form of rationalism that ironed geometry until it seemed
        to radiate
Wall studs and door posts and garden stakes and trees, tall girls, giraffes, and
        hierarchies in which the lowly look up
Their next moves. All this and more. Schopenhauer cuts vegetables
Willingly and even forcefully into floral figures over which he exerts
        romantic, voluptuary power
While the carnival lights of Ulm momentarily distract most burghers from
        the mighty cathedral rearing skyward
In crescendoed stone. How wondrously like rolling smoke are the façades
Forming! The thistle-field masks! Each forcing simplicity through a tube and
        out
Of whack. The crazier among us turn more and more frequently away from
        the center ring,
Where, oddly enough, the deepest divisions create and uncreate airless chasms.
It's out of these, gasping for breath, that clowns leap, and it's one of those,
        wearing pink and riding a blue horse that
Seems to be bleeding from every pore, who, in the throes of oxygen
        deprivation, switches hues with that horse, thereby earning
Wild applause, at least from the men who haven't fainted and the children

who (the only animals they know being those they've seen on the "Discovery Channel") don't understand

That animals on their own terms hoard increments of exhibitionism over many millennia, gradually shaping pragmatic maenad worlds of

Which little (in the modern world) gets seen. It goes on, of course, but who notices

The bravado of a box-elder bug except to brush it off, mentally and physically, as either mere chaos or mechanics?

Animal life picks up at night with the closing of the morning-glories. Mosquitoes and raccoons, privy to the secrets of lost time,

Pursue their macro-micro conquests, multiply measured by owls' wings, moving clouds,

Temperature shifts. On Wednesday night, for example (remember?), the dry winds ceased suddenly, as if giving up, and by midnight

Stillness matched darkness. What we noticed then was the wild dance of—it wasn't seeds so much as portions of

The daring shadows they were casting as they cast themselves in their fecund autumnal frenzy past feeding birds toward something both theirs and them:

The "knowledge" that, though they were greater than the sum of their parts, they were also

Curious and smart. Our memories, now, as if shadows of those shadows, revive

The realization that the "knowledge" of those shadows included a sense of being *smaller* than the sum of their parts, so that

We are humbled, and must admit our own insignificance—an irrelevance so complete that it can't be communicated to shadow or seed

Graciousness—unless the ancient grain-of-corn ceremony be tried

And the pas de trios (or pas de tous et toutes) be danced. Change of direction, of pursuit—even change of identity—though it may be fated isn't fatal

Until it is. I remember, too, reading about supposed death-and-back experiences and being bored

By the inanity of what was overheard on the way and the reluctance of the dying/not-dying to stay

Dead. Even though it represented an opening-out into light, space, magic,

The way through (as I saw it in my mind's eye) involved a long straight tunnel (similar to a concrete conduit), and the technological expertise

Required necessitated a doubling of security measures—measures? Two hands caressed the "conduit"

Amorously (or sometimes angrily) to render it roughly conducive
To phenomenological variation. Greasing the lover's psychic zoom lens was
Thrilling, as much to the lover as to the patient Venus flytrap at which he
          potently gazed.
It didn't matter that that gaze fought its way through thickening film; the
          very glaze became a sort of rampart
Past which love could progress only with the proper password—and love is
          always speechless, as
If to say, "I handle words but what I know is pause
Equivalent to the number one (of durable duration)." Revival
Of the music of the muscles seems to cause composition to mmm mm mmm
          multiply moonpie
By a prime number or suncake by ten. We mumble as we eat, or hum
But you wanted this as a sifting through politics, I think,
In hopes of finding a magic ring that's said to have been dropped a century ago
And watched as it whirled downward through alternate opacity and lovely
          lacerating light by
A curious fish, and a hungry one too, who swallowed it and swam 90 leagues
          north
In a nearly straight line (discounting the curvature of the Earth) until she/he
          could see the gate
Through which a rapacious gang of corporate CEOs had dragged history to
          its death
Egged on by the very addicts who would mourn (or flail) such ugly turn /
          stop / absence / absence, if
They could own the grave site and forget the dead in time again so as to turn
A quick profit, rotten eggs on a blue plate, or so it seems in this photograph
          that magically
Reveals the maggots writhing in their orifices. But one look at it is enough
To give pause to a pack of photons. Imagine their hurried conferences
And the concocting of alibis. One guy will prove with sand that he was at the
          beach, another will wheel out
A bicycle, as if that were evidence of health, stability, and a recent
          philanthropic trip to Scotland,
"Whose summers," he will say "are not all that bad." Life on the streets,
          meanwhile, for those without credit cards, credit, or cars
Is no more than belief in movement. Spectatorship disappears, except for an
          occasional red

Band of colored cloud materializing on (and as) the horizon at sunset, as
        hopes rise
Like helium balloons at a Fourth of July picnic. Goya's magpie topples over,
        afflicted by West Nile
Hieroglyphs as minute as the tiniest facets of an old Spaniard's personality
        and as feathery
As Mallorcan smoke. *Is* there life and talk *on* streets? "Try it,"
Says a passerby whose presence corresponds with a butterfly's
Name. He hops from one foot to the other so rapidly his legs look like a
        stationary cloud
Sketched on a largish drawing pad abandoned face up for now on a table
        barred by shadows cast by sunlight coming through the yellowing
        Venetian blinds
Of a middle-sized country house in one of Jane Austen's "lost" novels.
        Nevertheless
We're talking about the conflict between the "individual" and "society" in
        2005, and novelty
Is only the obvious secret advantage the individual might wield. Habit,
        novelty's spouse,
Wields secrets of its own, hidden in familiarity, like the ghosts of a house's
        past inhabitants
Might be mistaken for Sam next door, come to borrow a cup of sugar or
Look over the goods of the deceased—the pots, knives, books, albums,
        bedsteads, wall hangings, and "antiques."

Paddle

PADDLE

A paddle of dim rhubarb of. What do we owe to each other, what do we owe to ourselves? Wonder if the little Dinosaur Age mammals tended as brown or.

The elegy celebrated the history of her having flourished and the chance that we would flourish too. "Steve, why is that thing beginning to crack, do you suppose?" Life can't be studied as if it were nonlife.

Perhaps A Deer, Distilling Little Emergencies. It's not to express one's character (oneself) but to discover one's fate (one's happiness) that one acts. There's a fly on my nose—is it on yours too?

The new postal clerk ("Mrs. Thompson," according to her badge) is *intentionally* obtuse—expression blank, going slow, she devotes herself to frustrating the customers. A thunderclap arrives on a little scrap of wood on which one can barely pick out the painted letters "ndenbur." The melancholy collapse like puppets because they are unable to speak.

"Tishomingo Blues" sliding into the wild asparagus (dull green) … note for next spring. The apples on the tree are accurate and adequate to a summer day. I had to quit railroading / we didn't agree at all.

Jealousy frustrates one's plans for thinking back fearlessly—one's initial happy passivity is invaded. After Henry stepped on a rock which slid, causing Henry to fall and crack his knee, the rock was tried, convicted, and hung for inconstancy. We are so impressed within by war that our faithful cheer is disturbed.

Love / love love love love **WHAM** love love. I ended up waiting for the bus at night for half an hour, and while eavesdropping on her cell phone conversation, I made eye contact with a woman who was explaining to whomever was on the other end that she had to stop off at the Starry Plough to take in an Irish concert to fulfill the journalism class assignment requiring students to observe a crowd, and we cracked up. The sharper the angle (the closer to parallel with my line of sight) the more the dust on the window obscures what's out there.

I dreamed that there were no disjunctures, or none, at least, that weren't instantly filled. Wonder if the fucking space heater has any sense; beige "e" on my window, laughable. There is no defeat without outcome.

I really enjoy the movie *New Faces*, because when I first saw it fifty years ago it represented the initial in-the-flesh outside confirmation of a joke I had. The woman at the intersection was ranting at an imaginary interlocutor who, judging from what I overheard, seemed to be the CEO of an insurance company whom she had caught with his hand in the till. An announcer the other evening accused Nowitzki of the *Mavericks* of being, however good he is, a bit "mechanical."

It's impossible to ascribe absolute irrelevance to any sudden sound in the dead of night. I smell something, Jocko; you been eating horse puckey again? Gazing, gardening, counting other people's dough—that pretty much describes my life, says one young bank clerk to another, and the second bank clerk is like, yikes, you gotta come out with us, Mike, but he's waiting on someone and it's often like that, we've got our little baggies and our scraps of paper, maybe teabags and a bottle of water, a $20 bill, just to keep ourselves on the street that'll get us home, between the devil and the deep blue sea.

A very pretty maiden stood up and said, "Me look-look plenty quick goddamn big pirate Mistah Peter Burling me plenty baby!"; the Governor coughed discreetly. Tumblers the watch lets: their love of unstable equilibrium is demonstrated in their riding. Lapsed banshee of sail several through though tough a oops into unto and two.

Readily car, hurriedly dog, of butter of what of bump to our doom. But once again. "Milton produced *Paradise Lost* as a silkworm produces silk, as the activation of *his own* nature."

"Need and corp, end corp, (if truth on kid locks front mush hey move on back or mush) corporeal hole." The collection of sounds of words of the old father receives the benefit of a doubt which is otherwise of very slight use. Was the ribbon of cloud now precisely behind the jackdaw nest? Frances wondered.

Right forefinger on j, left pinky on a, left middle finger dipping to c, right middle finger on k, the typist works to write "jack" sure that Jack, left forefinger swinging right and reaching down, left pinky on a, left middle finger dipping to c, right middle finger on k, will write "back" back. Then the linnet in flight set its particle sight on the tongue's tip back of the waving feminine flax. But along comes a lovely night in May and the jolting jollity with which it's beginning can't but remind us that when time ticks through modernity, each tock comes as an awful shock, laughing though we may be.

So this fuckin' guy walks up and grabs my fuckin' jacket and says, "Who the fuck d'you think you fuckin' are?" and I spit in his fuckin' face; what the fuck. Marguerite had a headache and was ragging on everything she saw: the nose-picking clown pushing his way through the close-packed pedestrians, the glossy balloon adrift and headed for a tree, and the spectacular clouds overhead and in no position to judge. Please obtain surrogate indigo; thanks; it offers no trace of jollity; undesirable doughnuts get eaten.

I once had a plough horse—I didn't eat soup and lived in a trench and whenever my bad conscience troubled me, I wept until I could weep no more, which many found offensive. "There's the thoroughfare," expostulated Grimes, wiping his nose on a trouser cuff, flicking a rough look at Mrs. Houghton. The wind is advancing the trees, they are literally closer, it's hardly a wind—more like a breeze—but the branches are already pecking and scratching like birds at the windows.

Did any of you know that the root of "blame" is "blaspheme," as if irreverence were not a sign of tortured love but an ascription of some shameful responsibility? I'll translate: among the other animals aboard there are some cats, but alas not the scrawny black one—it was crushed by a tractor in Bordeaux. In the morning a friend of mine goes out and "flaps his wings" while looking at the light on Steve's sidewalk and the high, dead twigs.

Just above the pasture gate there was a deep ditch that we roofed over with scrap lumber and sod, and during the heat of the day we hid there, pretending to look at the stars, ignoring the whispered question that was perpetually asking if we were ready. What this means is that blue is a color, a lovely color combining surprise and endurance that is later found, sometimes, gleaming from coils of copper-based alloys and one must sort it out. Patty went canoeing and ran out of steam—neck and shoulders aching, arms limp, she drifted, dazzled by reflections (which are, as we know, materials from which a psychoanalysis might develop).

"How does this camera work?" asked Bob, smiling in a very strange way that made you think of a civet cat and a mongoose meeting, or almost meeting, in the surface (cheeks-and-mouth area) of a fair-skinned Swedish girl's face. I tossed all night with Verlaine fever, imagining that I'm being called Crescent by someone with a fishing pole named Mr. Ticket and I woke with a sense of guilt and an overwhelming fear of apologizing. The fundamental principle of quirky and unpredictable success by fortuitous side consequences pervades all scales.

The bucket stands under the faucet and is full and under the bucket there's a snake. Kawga / giwi hoobors—giwi hampo / mainorilp slitchab pusa / waldbro / hozrvaughn. The collagist sets a new blade into her matte knife, she selects an inch of light, her decisions have to convey the fact that reality is conditional, her blade rasps on the pad.

In a moment, it seemed, the pedestrian stepped on his own experience, and the experience, caught under the shoes, was pulled away—how fast that can go!—and, what else?, it started to snow. The son of Emawayish has opened the anisette-scented notebook of terminated songs. I thought, "Animism can't begin to account for the mess we're in," as the sun rose.

The team of agitated lame hunting dogs gave flight to every possible pleasure except that of rescuing one of them, the one I've named Since. After a few moments, Georgette began to los so o h fav fla an dre. Once there was a turtledove living in a tree, once there was an ornithologist who looked like me.

Tell it to the Chancellor of the Exchequer—he's right there! This has been called a painterly poem—it's a picture of the fleeting as well of the thing that flees, very much like one of the woodblock prints of the Japanese Ukiyo-e tradition: a picture of the floating world. "Gracious me," exclaimed Harriet, "we'll be late for the cheese sale!" (as Hortense compressed her lips and kept on randomly pounding the keys).

Bring on Tums and coffee, Rolaids and wine. Perhaps the most outstanding examples are furnished by the beaver, which employs aspen and birch in particular for construction materials as well as for food. Stand up, turn right, walk five paces forward, turn right again and pass through the bedroom whose door is now open and through which you'll see the stairs which I think you should descend and at whose bottom you should turn left and then left again, which will take you into the kitchen where you should immediately turn right, pick up a spoon, and stir the soup.

Now see here, Mr. Cowfrazen, it seems you—always—seem to hurt the very—uh—one that you love, with a hasty word you just can't seem to REcall. Powdery mist: erasure; Colonel Kernel; sour apples and approximate limes. Résumé résumé résumé résumé résumé.

I could name it the first word I thought when I woke if I could remember it. The nose-picking clown pushing his way through the close-packed pedestrians turns and smiles, "I'm number one." I'll stop here and put the rice on.

There are so many things in here I can barely see out, but the opposite is also true (melody, melody). Stress gives us grounds for comparing the tree tops with the Cyclops. "Is giwi hoobors an aphrodisiac?" chuckled Charlene W. Nervegas, chucking the thin chin of Chuck, her chuckwalla, in a "Wallace" cranny of the chuckwagon.

When loving cannot be composed any better, then loving cannot be postponed any longer. So I go make a cup of cold instant and think, "It's my turn." From the window it looked like the house nextdoor was in flames, but when I went out I saw that what was burning were only leaves on a maple tree.

"Bitte" seems sardonic, "please" a bit sleazy, "s'il vous plait" appropriate leakage. On the other hand, it could be *Jane* who's the thrifty one making rubberband balls and *Alice* who's the spendthrift with Marxist ideals. If we saw two sparrows in a narrow tree, how many mountain lions can dissolve a hill?

Between the fat man and the dirty woman stands the twitchy boy in a red shirt whom I take for a genius, though he's directing his remarks to the elevator door. 'Jever catch that nifty docu about gap-toothed women? The novelist, paraphrasing Descartes and without bothering to discover whether or not the people and places of which she writes actually exist, achieves a degree of certainty and an element of the indubitable.

Are you reading *Austerlitz Austerlitz* (which solves, at last, the problem of "Europe") and if not, why not?? whynotted Jack. The critic described the sound as "animal" but it sounded human to me, the critic called it "feral" but it sounded as if the utterer were sighing at the end of a dance, the critic called it "ghostly" but it sounded like a woman in a pasture under the shade of a tree. Wilson, enraged, sent a telegram to the Rajah: Waah wee wow umba ¢ mumba-p hik of thee nay-city.

The potter smiled at the turning pot, into whose clay he'd embedded a long red thread. At my left sat Florence Gingersnap; her eyes were pools of musk. Fur against glass, sun sucked by shadow, improvisation laboriously undertaken—we shudder with contrasts.

I'll have your Small Southern with sausage instead of ham, wheat toast, eggs over light. A girl on a horse on a stick whacking the doorframe enters the room and gallops through the socks. "Can't make one, leave a duck," said Wally and spat on the wood floor.

Here we are with bodies politic, yours a body politic and mine too, yours imitative, mine mimetic, yours classified, mine codified, yours minimized, mine assembled. Some blustering wind says we should marry. Along the same old lines, rumors surface.

As an Eastern European woman bellowed from the fifth floor window, "Could whozis be a cracker?" the teenage poet explained why he'd called his poem "No Numbers." One, shot of a shifty malingerer eyeing a covered basket; two, shot of 3 white kittens lapping milk; three, shot of protesters marching toward a castle: cannons roar, marchers fall. But I hardly think John knows enough about the history of navigation to, as it were, realize his way around the bedroom, much less escort the Duchess of Alba to, onto, on and off a suspicious-looking light blue train bound for parts south, at least this couple of years, do you?

Though I am writing this near an open window just past 7 one lovely evening in August, in my mind's eye it's raining in winter, a fly is dying on the windowsill, the golden curbside grass that's now being gently buffeted by the breeze is torn, tangled, brown, and soggy, and the cobalt sky is brown. As the whispering sex of the tick-infested goose. More even than film, and certainly more than music, dance, or painting, of all the arts we burden literature most with the task of answering to reality, either by improving it, or witnessing it, or transcending it, or describing it, or altering it.

Overheating could be due to a clogged hose, a heavily soiled dust compartment or exhaust filter, or a full dustbag. With the typical insomniac's predawn self-pity, the heroine of her own saga, which she knew to be sorry, tossed and sighed. Life is so full of a number of flyswatters I'm sure we should all be as happy as icewater.

"The negative" is right here with us, it's an experiential reality—the fissure through good sense via which the U.S. invaded Iraq. Bottle after bottle. Come rain or shine, you take the umbrella on even days of the month and I'll take it on odd and whomever the dog loves best, it will follow.

As I recall, the APC, or automatic pressure controller, was a silvery-looking thing, that simultaneously thrust and crouched, a thing of twirling screws until it settled into its mature form, and then it was a nest of hyper-responsive nuances. Linnaeus was fond of apes, and he couldn't concede to theologians that they had no soul. Then off it went, suddenly, toward the mountains, and Bobby began to cry.

"Loyalty is not a matter of signature." Even tying a shoe strains the very limits of the English language, as you will find if and when you seek to direct a Martian (even if he or she has, somehow, perfect English, and yet knows nothing of shoes) to the successful conclusion of that act. You're going to ruin your eyes reading in the dark, she said, dark eyes reading ruins, ruined eyes going dark.

Ha-ha ha-HA-ha, it's the Woody Woodpecker song. The mime hired by the cruise ship company to entertain the passengers so irritates one of those he mimics that one dark night the passenger strangles the mime and casts him overboard in an act of desperation he trusts will never be mimicked or mimed. Grainorelmamistoverguettewha-ilsysumkineujloaverts pcubfesque.

The black sweater with the yellow-wheeled red and blue train knitted into it still fits the boy and when it's outgrown it will fit the brother to whom he's coupled. When he walked into a room, even if it already contained a thousand people the room became an "Alexander sandwich." The carnivorous potted pitcher plant (1819) opened her pitchers when placed in the sun.

What she *heard* was: "Baby, Baby, please let me bake your bread." We watch a film flicking away what it films (the film "Dismissive"). On the other hand, Marjorie covered up every word of the present sentence with some eyebrow pencil she'd bought months, possibly years, before from Fred Martin around the corner from Safeway.

The toad, when interrupted, metamorphosed. She was born November 22, 1819, at South Farm, Arbury, Warwickshire, where her father was estate manager for the Newdigate family. Cultural life = social life, a life built of interactions, many of which are choice-driven (chosen) and many of which elicit choosing.

"My great aunt Edith had a mind like a porcupine," rumbled Stan as he pushed forward a checker which, Lothar saw in a flash that trailed regret, would be a sacrifice but would also trigger a retaliatory double-jump; the wet spot spread. The new monkeys, formerly said to be two feet tall but now described as "standing no higher than 16 inches," wake at dawn in Bolivia to embrace each other and, gazing into each other's eyes, they sing. Hydrochloric what?

Here we have a dream whose topography belongs to a different world, or perhaps it's a nightmare of magic words. NO LEFT TURN. After foresail comes foresee before it is foresaid.

The sawyer stops and wipes his brow; clouds like drifting whales; another hundred years rolls by. Beethovenian symphonies should erratically inspire the listener's unveiled sleepy walks through collapsing revelations toward a clear awareness of big poetry's thick, memorable, super-true spirit-shapes. At one time, Cimabue was the best painter in Italy.

A couple enters an upscale restaurant, they are shown to a table, he unfolds his napkin, she rests a finger on the base of an empty wineglass, a waiter brings a basket of bread, each respectfully examines the menu. Me go pickle-pickle Lewis MacAdams sewing machine blue jay down. The pizza goes in at ten of nine for a friend of mine who'll come in on time to eat it.

Each time I hold somebody new, my arms grow cold aching for you. In the writings of Colette (and privately perhaps in those of many women

diarists) quotidian sensation takes on meaning—takes it on and flaunts it.
All these realms are living systems in mutual interaction that display similar
patterns of self-organization, not unlike organic structures.

Not long after beginning to write, I continued to write, until more or
less later I stopped writing in order to read what I'd written—it was a copy
of something wonderful my mother had written. They were making the trip
by train, the southbound one o'clock, and Moira was meeting him at the
station. As the bats begin to swoop across the post-sunset horizon, Dick is
running his hand over the pink boulder precariously balanced at the edge of
the cliff overlooking the river.

Behind the abattoir, reading a manual, Bishop Berkeley blushed to
think what might happen next. The cunning vulture on the road we pass
(consuming gas) is cousin to the raucous robin on the grass. At last, after all
this, I discovered where the hatcheck girl lived; I smiled and tossed a pebble
at the second-floor window.

"This," says Bettina, pointing to what I call *a fork*, "is a turtle and I call
it Ilya Chin"—but on what grounds do I take "Ilya Chin" to be its name? The
other day I stood behind a woman with a snood, we were waiting to cross the
street, and when she turned she had a perfect Easter Island face. I hear sirens,
I listen more attentively, I go to the window, the sirens are getting louder,
I'm curious, I become aware of helicopters overhead, I want to know what's
happening, nothing unusual is visible, no smoke, no smell, just what it is that's
happening is unclear, I think of searching for it, determining what it is, I
decide not to, I'm disappointed but, mostly, relieved.

As Sandra McW. peered down from her blind high in a giant baobab,
the wild pig appeared from behind a blackberry bush and nosed its way
quietly, oblivious to the whir of the camera, across the clearing, wolfing the
strategically placed little sandwiches. Coming my way is a man's medium
forest green buffalo plaid from cyberspace. The Burgess Shale creatures
sported gills like tree branches, not even protected by a carapace, because
Archaeans came to dwell, publishing their popularizations (powered by
solar-remnant hot Earth center), and like a fugue the Hallucigenia, et al,
got straightened out, weaned into the breathless moderations of the world.

The alphabetical anemone thrives on a reef, attracting pretty prey to
its open vowels and shivering consonants. Cool it, Buster! Let's grant that
there exist in the external world, independently of us, entities of various
kinds among which are bees, settees, and frying pans.

"Do you want some of this Patak's Goan Pineapple Sauce on top or
not?" Mother, I want to get married. Earl Boykins is only five-foot-five;

he buzzes about in and through the other NBA players like a bee among robins.

The trading post lay in the distance like the shadow of a rabbit aware of a hawk and motionless, in imitation of a trading post. Finally the clouds turned yellow; Juanito smiled and went in for a bite. There are some things that everyone has to learn for her- or himself, things that others could tell them, but uselessly.

Uh-oh, a chip in the Natural History Museum mug (the white one). Mind in pencil to continue if so at all probably was. Sid said, "Solid," as the ship sank.

Wicker

WICKER

Let one line
of our poem
contradict
another!
(Walt Whitman)

One secret of
our sequence
is another.
(U.S. Grant)

I notice that
there is no
crescendo in our
narrative.
(Marina Tsvetaeva)

(The red throated loon
dives.)

I'll make a thousand
celestial observations
and render their
seeming eccentricities
consistent forever.
(Victor Frankenstein)

Until the rise of modern
dentistry (enabled by drugs)
most denizens had nothing
to smile with, or above,
and those who just up and
smiled anyway … idiots.
(Edward Dorn)

secrets, sequences
the poem better
haunted by its rocks
let's speak of night, thought
an outlaw species

when there's
an outlaw species
what laws can it
press from thought to night?
and rolling downhill

without looking
and rolling downhill
to kill until tomorrow
the sleepers curl and still
these night thoughts

roll on
these night thoughts
curve over a mass,
a species breaking from a
trough of numbers

audacity's a
trough of numbers
a chaos still precise
if we've time to think
of watching unawares

the root
of watching unawares
when "what-kind?" yellows "anyways"
is the quote the whereabouts
appears to broach

I made particular
friendship with one
huge tree.
(Zora Neale Hurston)

Let's have a beer.
(Robert Grenier)

The mouth
of the light-hearted
and reckless bee
hunter was instantly
closed.
(James F. Cooper)

When Jim Cox
learned his cows
and the Clinch River
didn't mix . . .
(William Stolzenburg)

Some readers may
object that we write
of things which have,
as yet, no existence.
(Margaret Fuller)

(And dives again,
but not as often as
comes up.)

Why this
unfathomable longing
of the soul
to vex itself?
(Edgar Allen Poe)

a violence
appears to broach
humanity, unable to fly
without fracture, and compelled by
the social moon

to mock
the social moon
in exile, with a
slightly ivory smile that cracks
open like chalk

and says
open like chalk
from mouths of deer
rocked in the passing air
but not here

implicate order
but not here
can't find a breach
can't find a two-dimensional bed
to slide into

tonight's wall
to slide into
while romancing with intelligence
takes writing's role in stimulating
an insinuating dream

somewhere inside
an insinuating dream
of California days sandwiched
between any two dark themes
unable to fly

the dream
unable to fly
(how does it think?)
wants its sleep sudden, a
cascade of birds

Another armored animal
—scale lapping scale
with spruce-cone
regularity.
(Marianne Moore)

I will lose myself
in the forest and turn
into a weasel
in a hole in a rock.
(The *Kalevala*)

Very slowly he squirms
by you and
you don't even know it.
(Rita Sansotta, grade 4)

A thing which has
utility is not a
thing of air but like
a blanket.
(Karl Marx)

Some to the sun their
insect wings unfold,
Waft on the breeze, or
sink in clouds of gold.
(Alexander Pope)

And there on the
platform I too had
debated, accents
staccato upon the pole.
(Ralph Ellison)

... his burning throne
... for men to gaze upon
The outside of her
garments were of lawn.
(Christopher Marlowe)

or song
cascade of birds
that rubs against the
spirit or its context until
it turns red

the darkness
it turns red
can't offend the science
we hold in our eyes
against the context

and I
against the context
against the opinions of
Husserl, take your science into
loosened fluid lens(es)

lights to
loosened fluid lens(es)
break the flooding dark
and from where I'm sleeping
scratch my neck

we think
scratch my neck
exemplifies a red turn
the shadow of the day
politics of Goethe

these Faustian
politics of Goethe
are sun dogs following
between aspiration and content
    desiring
volumes of light

blue entelechy—
volumes of light
verse in the dogtooth
violet band legend sublimn such
Santas of infinite

fallen in battle
a morally fallen man
delights in music
to speak at work
(Russian Reference Grammar)

LXII
Necklaces, neck laces,
necklaces, neck laces.
(Gertrude Stein)

You went swimming
in a Cadillac
like a duck down
in Los Angeles last
night in Athens.
(Rembetika)

On Jordan's stormy
banks I stand
and cast a wishful eye ...
(Alfred G. Karnes)

At evening with his
face to the huge sun
or his back I forget
it's not said.
(Samuel Beckett)

Delicious instants
before one's eyes get
used to the dark. Are
you still there? I said.
(Samuel Beckett)

I was there but
incognito, my hair black,
and I was smoking hash
into ash with a little
spark. (anonymous)

sleep—but
Santas of infinite
irrelevance and looping chores
band the night in sounds—
did you forget?

mirrored abyss?
did you forget,
dear, deep within my
heart is another heart? Audacity's
sudden valley capitals

kiss us—
sudden valley capitals
having burned our shadows
in a fit of madness
burn these words

to sanity
burn these words
to something sunny as
a scream, repeat the shadow
from another blink

great solace
from another blink
as vast as a dream
or whatever's thought's equivalent of
recurrent instant happiness

not possessive
recurrent instant happiness
that opens like chalk
on a black brass-mill floor
late afternoon shift

wanting the
late afternoon shift
from light to thing—
field condensed to leg, neck—
wanting more nights

Across the pale stillness
of water keel-carven, these
lovely eyes of desire
drag the ship to her doom.
(Simonides)

We only see
what we see
ourselves seeing
—ourselves seen.
(A. Dragomoshchenko)

But just then when I
took in any
inscape of the sky or sea
I thought of Scotus.
(Gerard Hopkins)

The ashes glittering
spears with their upright
stems—the hips very
beautiful, and so good!!
(Dorothy Wordsworth)

aaljsoidnoing
aojdoas
oinfg ag oias
(K. Blixen)

These indications
make us feel
how far removed we are
from all understanding.
(Edmund Husserl)

Houses were permanent and
they were framed with wood
or cane, by people who were
also boat builders.
(Carl Ortwin Sauer)

of love
wanting more nights
wherein magic overwhelms the
damn cathedral spread of simple
yellow, covered skin

exciting the
yellow, covered skin
in several inseparable places
with visibility, tension and rain
holding the light

rocked by
holding the light
haunted by infinite hits
of right, haunted by infinite
varieties of repetition

each night's
varieties of repetition
where people are bathing
their mysteries never the same
achieving flicker, hesitation

white space
achieving flicker, hesitation
hasn't ... flecked history with
its repeated white space which
pools so easily

and love
pools so easily
as nights go by
and the blind don't judge
the fortune-teller's future

as swimming
the fortune-teller's future
moves easily through crystal
deaf to the knocks of
light brown contingency

I drop honey in distinct
drops laid on stone and
then I retire carefully to
watch whether bees come.
(J. H. St. John Crevecoeur)

Doesn't one always think
of the past in a garden
with men and women lying
under the trees?
(Virginia Woolf)

Men and women struggling
in boundless perfectibility
choose to be sad but
to think without horror.
(Florence Hall)

O daughters of Mnemosyne
…
(it had begun to rain)
(Ovid)

Sudden transitions, inter-
mediate states between life
and death, simultaneous
peace and motion—all here.
(A.K. Zholkovsky)

whether he was rolling
that pellet of dung in
which ancient Egypt beheld
an image of the world.
(Jean Henri Fabre)

It is anchored
in all my questions and
answers, so anchored
I cannot touch it.
(Ludwig Wittgenstein)

this temporal
light brown contingency
and sense of modesty
—atomic or horsehair or rhythmic—
coincides with nothing

much, but
coincides with nothing
itself synchronizes, nakedly, with
"is eaten by remorse" wherein
the clothes merely

clothe us—
the clothes merely
speed into another sleep
our souls, always our copies
ignoring us completely

our configurations
ignoring us completely
like a sulfur-globe illustrating
magic at cost of fact
we can see

the fact
we can see
but in the dark
(and that makes three) rests
beside another face

a reference
beside another face
perfectly itself but cocked
at an angle, winging it
to be sure

and wanting
to be sure
we feel for it—
feathered, hot, corrugate or green
—trusting this evidence

Use it your way,
one line for each entry.
Strike a balance as often
as you find necessary.
(World Savings checkbook)

We love to expect,
and when expectation
is gratified) we want
to be expecting again.
(Samuel Johnson)

but of course
a can of quartz
&
I know you
(Shiki)

This prose poem
distinctly shows
the influence of
Rimbaud.
(anonymous annotator)

… no ideas
but in things …
(Neanderthal Man)

I know very well
we should celebrate
rather than regret
this absurdity.
(Panama Butler)

and the rose closes
upon the
stem
(Nancy Hill)

isn't entirely
trusting this evidence
it's snapping answers from
the untouchable, based in triangulation …
a lonely slave

to whatever
a lonely slave
is slave to, held—
grasped and only later released—
and sleeping free

as "gray"
and sleeping free
achieving flicker, hesitation hasn't
(one, two) these night thoughts
one empty hand

held in
one empty hand
habitually sheltered in sleep
under the sleeper unobserved, the
world hidden lengthwise

without measure
world hidden lengthwise
to measure desire now
neither tadpole nor a flagpole
the inhaled universe

drawn into
the inhaled universe
to measure, but how?
more pieces than ever, more
increments, rivers, flags

and especially
increments, rivers, flags
getting added to, until
the flow is like a
flow of flowers

we must pull our passions
through the hedges
to reserve confining
us to patience.
(Luther Burbank)

Measure the space in
the room,
then go ahead.
(Allen Ginsberg)

Moan hither, all ye
syllables of woe,
from the deep throat
of sad Melpomene!
(John Keats)

When the pie was opened,
The birds began to sing.
Now wasn't that a dainty
dish …
(Mother Goose)

I would gladly
have put off the
sentence still
on my mind.
(Louis Zukofsky)

The list poem (… "catalog
verse") is an excellent way
to introduce children … to
the writing of poetry.
(Larry Fagin)

No sound of any storm
that shakes … now
September makes / An
island in a sea of trees.
(E.A. Robinson)

and every
flow of flowers
is without outer limit
but folds and fruits in
sensations of suspense

the very
sensations of suspense
several times a day
that sever the mountainous
    horizon's
semblance of water

each night's
semblance of water
submerging order, absorbing day
floods each day's vanishing point
we look into

it but
we look into
its staccato units soft
or not finding their irregular-
ness a coastline

dreaminess can
ness a coastline
where elements from Monday
fit dramas along the cliffs
to no end

including soil
to no end
smearing night on chaos
like this, like that, like
oil on toast

nocturnes turning
oil on toast
dirty us in chasing
two men in blue suits
whom we catch

Washington crossing the
Delaware: *He saw his
ragged Continentals
row.*
(Dmitri Borgmann)

Suddenly a sailfish
leaped, straightaway
over these lines—
told in a splash.
(Zane Grey)

"You ar' an old settler in
these districts, then? …
nearly to overflowing …
delicious hommany …
prepared by his skilful,
though repulsive, spouse.
(Fenimore Cooper)

& the main thing is
we begin with a white
sink a whole new language
is a temptation.
(Bernadette Mayer)

To plot just these
seven loops required
500 successive calcu-
lations on the computer.
(James Gleick)

But let me stop you
for a moment—before
you go too far.
(Jacques Derrida)

sight of
whom we catch
in chaste pursuit, knocking
at 2:30, 4:30, creeping twilight
laced in knockabout

we too
laced in knockabout
and bound in flare
bound ahead unchastened,
        undressed, insomniac
unconquered, convicted, wolfish

—to be
unconquered, convicted, wolfish
(sharky) in these circumstances
shows "ride on the Reading"
incongruity to be

surpassed by
incongruity to be
taller than I when
I (or my equivalent) jut
elbow against tree

brave juniper
elbow against tree
Bernstein, snake musical, (bing!)
the minute I open my
face the music

and words
face the music
and all the singers
(who've dressed in my presence)
decry the war

Which you can
when a moment's gone
for all I care.
(Josephine Baker)

Oh! penetrating to the
point of pain I fill
the depth of the sky
with consternation!
(Charles Baudelaire)

But then
everything cools out
again.
(Werner Heisenberg)

I fall into
the icy water, not
humiliated but
silenced.
(Aphra Benn)

You gotta slide into
third as if you're
setting out to bury
yourself.
(Muddy Ruel)

New world giants
in Paul Bunyan's day
ate raw stallions
but it bored them.
(Priscilla Mastress)

A snapshot, developed &
framed. Being washed &
dusted, unable to sneeze.
Touched falling crash cut
replaced. (Bo Crofoot)

along the
decry the war
and the war's breath
that pushes until no atom
of absence remain

the ghouls
of absence remain
flickering in black and
white to make a show
of lifelike expressions

but cars
of lifelike expression
cruise the lines; one
flicker, then another, taps telephone
poles, translation overload

downs the
poles, translation overload
girds the white circles
to get the same smile
as marks thought

parenthesis, dash
as marks thought
with greasy red strokes
and one second of trickery
ghouls of absence

fooled by
ghouls of absence
with their legendary appetites
and their inappropriate good will
showing them up

ha! ha!
showing them up
the stairs into actual
cells, cracks stuffed with peach
pillows and straw

Or find us, deep within
some mine. Those famous
flowers, almost stones.
(Arthur Rimbaud)

Mir gefaellt Fra
Filippo Lippi
nicht.
(Phyllis Wheatley)

How sad young Ed looked,
having lost the pearls by
which he had assured his
place in our untidy gang,
I will not try to describe.
(Daniel Defoe)

Aspects of the spirit
accumulate on shore
… my grandmother calls
me by shaking the pans.
(Jamaica Kincaid)

All sorts of men through
various labors press
To the same end, contented
quietness.
(Lucy Hutchison)

Whitely, while benzine
rinsings from the moon
dissolve all but the
windows on the mills …
(Hart Crane)

There is an occult
relationship between
the scorpions
themselves and me.
(Ralph Waldo Emerson)

now plucking
pillows and straw
daylight shrinks into stars
steeled against justice or love
—but I'm lucky

no care!
—but I'm lucky
to be alive, a-love,
livid with a lack of sun,
a closed system

asleep, dreaming—
a closed system
of recognitions without feeling
although in the dream someone
("I") is laughing

because the
("I") is laughing,
fingers touching the back
(20c), the content, or is
it the hip

yes, call
it the hip
the leg a lip
the touch is *this* word
on "your" bird

which "drums"
on "your" bird
as an electric rodomontade
melting into all the literature
of particle theory

releases arpeggios
of particle theory
into anything we say
expanding the objects we speak
of into "mothers"

whack to lager law
wove papes
landau cuts rolled hotel
are so brimmage
(Clark Coolidge)

The mountain appeared
like an Angel with a
sword telling us to
stop and turn around.
(Etel Adnan)

Women slapped cunts on
their foreheads. A man
pinned one to his bicep …
(Jennifer Heath)

But the action produced
an effect altogether
unanticipated. The rays of
numerous candles now fell …
(E. A. Poe)

Often one may actually see
whippoorwills by driving
slowly along unimproved
roads and watching for the
orange "eye shine."
(Andrew Berger)

It is not because of
the dark that light
exists but rather it
is true of its own accord.
(Hans Blumenberg)

changing think
of into "mothers"
of intention, broadsides of
prepositions that we're read to
out of for

melodramas read
out of for
the sake of science—
juxtapositions of curios, monstrosities,
       comparisons,
lovers' quiddities, clichés

(not clinches)
lovers' quiddities, clichés
like—the word "cliché"
which turns repetition's subtle craziness
to sane distaste

taking love
to sane distaste
which history itself disdains
(what taste distastes turns sweet)
will unmake love

and beds
will unmake love
undo it till it
runs about the infinite coastline
in and out

searching, lonely
in and out
the ornithology, eyes closed,
hearing birds' experimental songs that
light can't register

As in a song, it is the
voiced elements of a poetic
line which bear onward the
line's main melody and help
to shape it.
(Douglas Oliver)

That's an identification:
a rail. Where? I hear its
song. Why privilege the
eyes? The ears are accurate.
(Jack Collom)

very much
like *"Earliest"*
in form
but *very*
much later.
(Luther Burbank)

Beyond this zone
conditions change very
rapidly—the deep-scattering
layer often giving the
impression of a false bottom
(P.B. Moyle & J.J. Cech, Jr.)

… part of the whole
from which love seeks to
contrast knowledge with
separation, and certainty with
the temporal.
(Lyn Hejinian)

They say in that country, We
esteem that woman because she
is chaste, as we say here, We
esteem her because she is
kind. And yet …
(Sir Joseph Banks)

we know
light can't register
it's far too swift
a song'd be a mass
of eternal width

a miss
of eternal width
and a plank path
(a sane distance) dividing it
and then what?

water reassembles
and then what?
the ripples of insanity
do slash, melt and weld,
begin planting green

greens themselves
begin planting green—
my attention is captured,
I can hardly turn away,
nothing means more

to me
nothing means more
to me, but—here's
a turaco-bird photo whose color
alternately becomes background

what's birdlike
alternately becomes background
and detail when what's
wordlike in microtude's
    magnificent song
matches this scale

So and so, toe by toe, to and
fro they go round, for they
are the ingelles, scattering nods
as girls who may, for they
are an angel's garland.
(James Joyce)

It is impossible to round
the globe from pole to pole
because the poles of the
other world, joined to
those of this, prevent it.
(Margaret Cavendish)

Entropy? Yes, indeed. Set
it down. Right there. I
can take it or
leave it alone.
(Sir Isaac Newton)

Between the posts of passion
extends a fence, and behind
the fence is a cow, and
overhead both suns are
shining.
(No one)

If you don't believe I love
you, look what a fool I've
been; you don't believe I'm
sinkin', look what a hole
I'm in.
(Gus Cannon, et al)

All historic anxiety, all
poetic anxiety, thus
torments this poem
of the interminable question.
(Jacques Derrida)

and drop
matches this scale
so twitter is atoms'
nervousness expanded to star
    cluster,
looking upward from

these omens
looking upward from
memories as they occur
are just twitters but more
just than twitter

alone which
just than twitter
I mean, the tumble
makes them logic's logo, as
the white pyramid

melts into
the white pyramid
the memorable logician situates
as ice (let's say so)
under our feet

well put
under our feet
slowly letting us down
every dignity we ever eked
from endlessness exposed

I retreating
from endlessness exposed
regret doing so, wish
the dignity (though ever eked)
out of control

I shatter the words …
that I put in a
sort of dangerous associated
system
I love.
(Melissa Kawecky)

… though you were never
to be loved again, if
you lived another time you
would contemplate it long …
(G. Apollinaire)

Opposites are alike
in every way but
one.
(Calvin)

In these days one person
cannot follow another
into sleep, as was the
custom long ago.
(Marie-Catherine D'Aulnoy)

forgive me for being blunt
I don't even believe in the
Milky Way.
(Nicanor Parra)

Yodeling is the least
aggressive but most effective
medium for declaring one's
belief in the existence of
distance.
(Oliver Messaien)

into and
out of control
like a wave that
never falls asleep; each reply
is its own

feminine—that
is its own
and its masculine too,
so I can't regret anything,
dear, after all

but how
dear, after all,
it is to praise
spinning fantasies out of philosophy
and vice versa

invisibility's marvels
and vice versa
are sensible—sleep's not
the moat around the tower
—it's the flower

trust me
—it's the flower
into which a beak
thrusts and there unseen sips
sleep's concentrate, its

flight around
sleep's concentrate, its
trustworthy coordinate, merging day's
many colors into nocturnal plum-
and lemon-yellow dream

Imagine a baby
in a field of grass ...
(Stan Brakhage)

He started from the
ground and threw around
himself a look of dear
but desperate eagerness.
(Anne Radcliffe)

ah fond memories of the nut-
house/ with its cracked
leather chairs/ its view of
the Seekonk River
(Aimee Grunberger)

In large Rivers, the Ice is
burst by imprisoned Vapours
with a Noise not less
terrible than the firing of
many Guns.
(Christopher Middleton)

1 large onion
1 lemon
½ teaspoon sea salt
½ teaspoon freshly ground
black pepper
(Amadea Morningstar)

chop the onion, squeeze the
lemon, mix with olive oil,
garlic, tomato and basil and
stir into cooked pasta; top
with avocado marinated in
more olive oil and lemon
(*S.F. Chronicle)*

diverging paths,
and lemon-yellow dream
seems to lead reconnaissance
into the thinner hypnagogic film
half-black and half

invisible or
half-black and half
only, of what was—
knowledge of this is never
the same again

because being
the same again
means something too static
for knowledge. Foreknowledge, for
    example
is a slant

as th'hypotenuse
is a slant
but incommensurate with hills
in landscapes or hills in
the word hills

or with
the word hills
that is, the hills
composed of words, like dirt
(rock or clay)

in sentences
(rock or clay)
with which we say
the world is this way
subject before object

So much liquid music
to be heard
but love is just
a four-letter word …
(Robespierre)

Often rebuked, yet always
back
back returning
To those first feelings
that were born with me …
(Emily Brontë)

I woke and chid my honest fingers,—
The gem was gone;
And now an amethyst remembrance
Is all I own.
(Emily Dickinson)

Dickens was fond of excess
using it frequently to increase
enthusiasm for a tale he was telling
in parts.
(Abraham Fraunce)

Holly, mistletoe, red berries,
ivy, turkeys, geese, game,
poultry, brawn, meat, pigs,
sausages, oysters, pies,
puddings, fruit and punch,
all vanished instantly.
(Charles Dickens)

As we proceed with our
investigation we come to
words which can no longer
be defined.
(Blaise Pascal)

does not
subject before object
object to static "role"
passivity, whereas it has unquenchable
energies, like static

electricity and
energies, like static
space in active time,
communicate the independence of the
object (even this)

which doesn't
object (even this)
to thought being like
an Africa-thinned daughter, fresh,
        unpronounceable,
setting up practice

night's practitioners
setting up practice
apply reason to imagination
for the swifter, surer shifting
of the will

the daylight
of the will
is causing each item
one describes discrete in space
to be discrete

writing's arrangement
to be discrete
sets episodes to stories
or provides examples for explanations
but what dreams!

… and yet you incessantly
stand on your head.
Do you think at
your age it is right?
(Lewis Carroll)

One cannot be right
and be indifferent, too;
this being true, to be
different is to be right.
(Clara Regla)

Dawn is but reflection, and
how can I be different
when I am everything,
I ask you.
(Sue Person)

like wondering what will
happen if you get famous—
haven't you been preparing
for this all your life?
(Steve Benson)

It is a felt insistence on
the present in such a text
that gives narrative or
semantic indeterminacy a
"positive" value.
(Reed Bye)

The discrepant shadows of
that *are* its meaning, lengthening
excessively now over
the body, the only presence.
(unattributable)

constantly waking,
but what dreams
must daily plod white
hours, hours, the practice sessions,
reversing the order

dreams repeat,
reversing the order
the source draws closer
to a purple cardboard rooster
from the street

in time
from the street
is to be discrete
in rhyme, then invite a
real yellow hen

and that
real yellow hen
pecking at bright blindspots
sees into the click between
curiosity and this

uncertainty, if
curiosity and this
darker copy of itself
can keep entropy happy playing
with y-ending words

that embody
with y-ending words
the gay century, near
unity now, its plenty displayed
but yielding yet

The lycanthrope phenomenon
is merely curlicues of
general intensity, when
intensity confronts social
stricture and, beyond that,
wild numbers.
(Mme. Maria Ouspenskaya)

A woman whom a man did not
want to love went to a zoo.
This happened in a story
called "The Buffalo."
(Helen Cixous)

Poetry is a slow flash
of light because it comes
to you piece by piece.
(Felix Rivera)

But nothing's perfect, the
alien document you open
is text—just text—
until midnight—which
is here.
(D.G. & R.W.)

Try one—we won't laugh!
Beartooth
Blueberry Lager
$3.00 bottles
(Sundown Saloon)

Poetry responds to this
appropriation of experience
and leaves the animals
dumbstruck.
(L.H.)

to backwardness
but yielding yet
another turn too, to
your typical ply, your play
wandering back through

great seriousness
wandering back through
the comedy of alphabet
whose letters match sound's throttles,
confidences, and squabbles

it's like
confidences and squabbles
coincide, while full throttle
(top speed or totally choked)
trafficjams of truth

reach gridlock
trafficjams of truth
wheeling atonal platitudes producing
boredom instead of strokes in
place—*this* place

is a
place—this place
is filled with variant
images of its own motion
leading to a

circle, argument
leading to a
longing to telephone, explain
how mind's "something" (alphabet) itself
longs to explain

A magnificent rainbow
Bellowed the sky with rays of color
Cast the beautiful fairies
Dawned the twilight's mist ...
(Sadie Babits, grade 4)

A man was stung by a bee
today, which offered romance.
The man confessed. Thus we
see that romance is not
always escapist.
(The Woman)

Repeat that, repeat ...
Off trundled timber and scoops of
    the hillside ground, hollow hollow
    hollow ground:
The whole landscape flushes on a
    sudden at a sound.
(Gerard Hopkins)

The tongue must lie on the
floor of the mouth except for
a very slight arching about
midway between front and
back.
(Margaret Prendergast McLean)

The legal profession *is*
a massive abdication of
responsibility.
(Bill Campbell, in conversation
    outside a hardware store)

Now let me tell you
a fairy tale or two
to make you feel a
little better.
(Apuleius)

shows and
longs, to explain
how they make music
the ribbon of continual imperfection
laughing, correcting itself

adding notes,
laughing, correcting itself
so nothing's left out
and if it's too loud
be lazy, nap

below, above
be lazy, nap
a downy surface, sip
a tawny port, land, climb down,
look all around

our lives
look all around
nothing's ever the same
but suddenly funny and scary—
it is uncanny

and pinched
it is uncanny
how the walls create
a rush, a crush of difference
between now and

Thisbe or
between now and
Pyramus—through their fingers
slips the wall they whisper
through, inside out

First, some simplicities that
a man learns, if he works in
OPEN, or what can also be
called **COMPOSITION BY FIELD**
as opposed ...
(Charles Olson)

To the flying wish and
small wonder lower on
the same page, an aphorism:
a total is an impudent frame.
(anonymous)

Sunlight
contains a buzz
Softness is as softness
does.
(Emily Dickinson)

I start to descend
then decide to fall
instead; en route
I regret not going
by foot from the start.
(The "Engine Man")

A small picture presented
the interior of an immensely
long and rectangular vault or
tunnel, with low walls,
smooth, white, and without
interruption or device.
(Edgar Allan Poe)

We had reached the goal but
the return was still before
us, a white circle of light
just visible through the ice.
(Robert Peary)

they die
through, inside out
Babylon, where cuneiform has
wedged money, love and war
into the clay

nights pressed
into the clay
as afterthoughts, dream clefts
between fallen lips meshed vast
outlasting flower points

in dazzle
outlasting flower points
under the rise of
archaeology; the very 'clature conjures
a noisy collapse

in ruin
a noisy collapse
intellectually accomplished,
    emotionally reserved
with the traits of coral
at sleep's onset

a fish
at sleep's onset
swims between red rims
often, repetition drawing dream context
to a maelstrom

down horizons
to a maelstrom
dropping its cavorting coast
down concave cliffs to paradise
that hazy boundary

a point moving along this
trajectory in phase space
illustrated the slow, chaotic
rotation of a fluid.
(Edward Lorenz)

curls tight
that hazy boundary
of light to lightness
like a dust-devil made of
nerves and loam

One moment of daylight let
me have Like a white arm
thrust Out of the dark and
self-denying wave And ...
('Ern Malley')

the unconscious
nerves and loam
devil the threaded night
and thrust ('earthy' spring dream)
to finger roots

We now know that the paleo-
escapment was *not* the natu-
ral edge of a reef, but a
"mega-truncation surface" of
a giant underwater collapse/
spiralling-off of the cathe-
dral carbonate platform.
(Christopher Collom)

of how
to finger roots
that simply rub spice
against the sky like a
patient acrobat, one

kayuk: it's the end
kayur: dog- or reindeer-team driver
kayut: cabin
kayushchiicya: repentant
(Russian)

stirred, bound
patient acrobat, one
spread between two rings
of love and flying out
to pull chestnuts

Look, look, the dusk is growing.
My branches lofty are
taking root. And my cold
cher's gone ashley. Fieluhr?
Filou! (James Joyce)

(last cabins)
to pull chestnuts
out of thick red
books, like a dog-team driver
without a home

Our feeling for reality depends
utterly upon appearance,
thus we must believe in
whatever appears out of the
dark.
(Hannah Arendt)

exiles, wanderers
without a home
cross the night border
telling tales of wrinkled flirts
telling tales themselves

in London in fall, mist and fog.
E. P. in B. M. tea-shop says
Hermes, Orchard, Acon
will 'do.'
(H.D.)

I dream that my shoes
have been glued to
the floor of a convention
hall and I am in them.
(A Dreamer)

Whaddya mean? Whaddya
mean? Let's go down ta
Minsky's. I believe it's somewhere
on South State Street.
(Chicago Johnny)

As a way of testing this
scene, let's return to the
ledge where the men and
women are luridly juxtaposed.
(Jane Tompkins)

M'boy, there's endless
space in the shadow
of the leading edge.
(Marie Curie)

Perhaps the hideous
animals were overcome by
panic and ran upright
in the course of the fire.
(Georges Bataille)

I would concede that he might
have contented himself with
testing it in the shallows.
He did, after all, survive.
(Jane Wodening)

castoff clothes
telling tales themselves
a twitch for every
denouement, odors wrapping up the
basic clash chiaroscuro

of woolen
basic clash chiaroscuro
and progressing itchy innuendo
between admirer and regardless flirt
fucking with bugs

but then
fucking with bugs
implies a Steinesque repetition
I mean each move slightly
alters the pattern

milky idleness
alters the pattern
of night's designated apathy
but a sunny slap draws
an asymmetrical fury

which twirls
an asymmetrical fury
which burrows into the
almost-liquid slow whirlpool dimly
        contained
at an angle

repetitions withdraw
at an angle
alter complaint, producing nightmares
from which one shudders up
condemned to sunflowers

as draft
condemned to sunflowers
though their embryo nods
might stalk and stalk and
never actually arrive

… holding his being
independent of his passions.
I affirm, however, in terms
of these passions.
(as if Georges Bataille)

And the days are not full enough
And the nights are not full enough
And life slips by like a field mouse
Not shaking the grass.
(Ezra Pound)

"Quiet grass, quiet grass,"
says the mouse; "if only you
were full you could stop this
day and night and make me
an eternity."
(Fairy song)

… parasitized by tiny
sucking fish. It was not
discovered until rather re-
cently that those miserable
parasites were the males of
the species!
(Robert A. Wallace)

But it need not be a male at
all; there was a long tunnel
undercutting my grandfather's
house and we cut it ourselves
—Anya and I.
(I myself, hiding for weeks on end)

limb, tibia, fibula, shinbone,
shank, garn, peg, pin, stump,
calf, thigh, ham, support,
prop, brace, post, column,
hotfoot, skedaddle
(J.I. Rodale)

rising smokes
never actually arrive
to thumb the eyes
—through the funning 9 smudge
I look forward

and backward
I look forward
with an 8, backward
with a 7, sidestroking in
the melted ice

upended on
the melted ice
you've got my number
which is added to or
subtracted from yours

@ %
subtracted from yours
when looked at becomes
place = motion but never
the twain shall

meet, twin—
the twain shall
never do that—imagine
saying the twain shall walk
—we went walking

then hopping—
we went walking
and the rule was
all of our legs had
to touch at

Here is a sketch of eye-
glasses—two circles joined
by a crossbar—so it must
be a bicycle or maybe two
buckets on a yoke.
(A.R. Luria)

Because there is Friction be-
tween the balls, a cueball
with left-hand spin will
grip the object ball for an
instant and throw it off-line
to the right.
(Robert Byrne)

I burst into tears and
stretching my hands appealed
to the humanity of the
audience; but no one would
raise even a finger to help me.
(Apuleius)

"my own end?" "But the
yellow eyes multiplied,"
"became so numerous" "that
the blackness was covered
over" "by them"
(Alice Notley)

The gigantic eye of Tolstoy
opens and closes many times
and at many doors—a kind
of primitive wooden flicker.
(Barrett Watten)

Other names: Yellow-shafted
Woodpecker; Golden-winged
Woodpecker; Clape; Yellow-
hammer; High-hole; Yarrup;
Wake-up; Wood-pigeon; Heigh-
ho; Wick-up; Hairy Wicket;

reflections moving
to touch at
themselves, so we went
wading in a river with
clear optical echoes

see? see?
clear optical echoes
e-c-h-o
that's really just one of
them, one of

us, imitating
them, one of
them having turned into
a bird; but it's turning
out of it

and into
"out of it"
itself—the century lays
an egg; Coyote Chronos cracks,
sucks it up

wonders who
sucks it up,
self-consciousness not being his
impediment to act or age
as it's ours

and hours
as it's ours
and years to suck
a Middle-Ages *donjon* rampart
  made
of crushed labels

Yawker-bird; Walk-up.
(*Birds of America*, T. Gilbert
Pearson. ed.)

I see a woodpecker and then
know that my body's a piece
of wood. I'm stroking the
dog and then I know that this
dog's gonna bite my feet.
(Dave Van Ronk)

Soon the puddle of words is
gone and then, boom, another
puddle is there, and I have
to set them free. I really
do love it when it "snows."
(Chris Wilson, Leadville)

Voyagers in absent
landscapes know nothing
of the women who stroll
along the invisible
embankments made famous
in their own poetry.
(Charlotte Jones, Turlock)

Disparities between the
energies of oxygenation and
gravity are responsible for
most cardiac inflammation.
(Dr. W. P. Wechselgeld)

Go on to something else.
Give up. Proceed. You will
turn right and walk along
the windowsill, the shore,
the sea.
(Marguerite Duras)

and labors
of crushed labels
we domesticate as walls
that suggest art to literary
or scientific intellectuals

not religious
or scientific intellectuals
because their dimensia angle
into angels, either of glimmer
or of gold

of intermediaries
or of gold
uncertainties represented by
    manifestations
of vivacity among feathered women
we know much

soft? hard?
we know much
of the bodiless changes
like checkerboard capes tossed over
the cold taffrail

ice coats
the cold taffrail
gripped by an inquisitor
weak at the (soft? hard?)
towering sea wall

And what's romance? Usually
a nice little tale where you
have everything As You Like
It, where rain never wets
your jacket …
(D.H. Lawrence)

And someone needs someone
and that someone wants "to
have a look" in a melancholy
way—so the results are
… well … voyeuristic?
(don't go away!)

(every happiness of other
making being destined to dis-
appear into the shades of the
predetermined nothingness of
the self-claiming self,
which encircle it)
(Laura Riding)

O you
towering sea wall
she cries, do not
crash down on me until
we finish questioning

the one
we finish questioning
in panels, sequels, nights
the sea cups, eye buckets
and we scale

the heights
and we scale
them down to variable
peckerwood shadow plays that
  make
the poem better

Sunflower

SUNFLOWER

Sunflower just below gray cornucopia roof
The usual guard from the spirals
Of the day / the horn's justice
And knot; the horn's whistle
Verbalizes, bounced light breaks down the
Silver clods of shoveled chime, the slipping out of
Hedge and in again. Customers
Are Nietzsche, every one, and in their suffering
Hair are flames of space (like this) half-beaten
Just as morning is menacing if one wakes, ambivalent, too late
To circle rapidly in white lightbeams, but
Made for signaling a response. Talk of plots and sentimentality
Strings and cools the sentimental plans
To keep words constant. But what colors are
Dots syntax into a cherry bow (cherrywood bow)
Attached to melodramas acted out by clocks (do I mean clouds?)
Clattering, light green. The horn's whistle's white streak
Is grammar's worm, morning's light. Winter's slippage
Down through amusing scallops barely averts denudation
And its consequences—nudity and unity.
Whose shadow is that, across the counter
Moving against mine? The book of prose skies is open
To die cat's-paw *sans* linebreaks, like tills, although
A moment later not like this at all. Stages of experience
Follow curves of surface tension up / down to the next
Letter. Dear Jack,
I wanted to ask, how did this English salutation come in
Like a sunflower "volunteering"? An invitation with its consequences
Spilling over and auspicious, standing up for, or, rather, flying at
A word into an aperture, the sun, which draws the blue.
Dear Lyn, if heaven adds increments and knowledge undulates
We must logically and carefully suppose.
Finis. Meanwhile, that shoveled chime's shimming
Adjusts, aligns—or no, uplifts—or, no, upholds—the studs, and then the barriers
(Tweaked) break out. And we have what we have
And everywhere we want to go for sunflowers we can go.

But when it comes to yellow birds, the impulse turns
To music, and then the scientist arrives and writes the following:
"I see that I don't see, or, rather, a pale smear appears
On the smudge I've called the sky, not wanting it to end, *it-bird, it-sky,*
        regardless of my eye
'S regard—regard—regard. Crash." That tune ends, and
I find myself thinking of the butcher at the grocery store whose name is
        Raymond Jones, of his white clothes
And the spots before his eyes he tells me of, and the fair land
At noon in its smoke, and fat bears, unanimous chrysanthemums (but
        towards what do they bend their unanimity?), and children
        hammering fantasies into plums
And pears. From the cornucopia some whistle emerges; I smile at the delicate
        gray
Cement and the words written on the wall which say "We are the wall by
        being here."
Then they say, "Top branches bare in cycle logic," then subside, spilling slightly
Into the panorama. Philosophy ought to hesitate, use commas when it uses
        words,
So continuance's spirit, at least, might, yes, fleece,
Spiral, or weave. The sun is already divided
Into a hundred arcs, variant versions of itself, clubbed in the positive
And banding in the negative, just as late yesterday, in muddled silence,
All these movements stood on top of each other, teetering, pale
As the words "jeremiad" and "idiosyncrasy." At night in fall the sunflowers
Are filtered through sounds like "Husserl" and arrive a little bluer
Than the sky, though "pure consciousness" encountering "the appearance of
        things" may cloud
The sunflowers, uns*lf worse, into "ur-owl-ness (f)"
(The word itself fouls wrens) and the iron shelters for the border guards
        bound by the strands of rain.
A moment of silence. Then a rise to the top of things: the ever-present tiny
        leaps:
The links (as late as yesterday). Today it really rained, or something else
        repeated,
If the rhythm of real / unreal is really repetition. I was eating eggs
And anticipating (anticipation is always dependent on the senses)
A spunkier texture than I'd been used to, whereas each new parenthesis
        paused to introduce … a joke, nothing structural,

Although contingent—sudden, but to the point—or, rather, now that I
　　　　think about it, missing the point, but intentionally, so as to defer
As it were, the bestowal of a middle name on Relativity Theory, and all the
　　　　attendant
Dissipation, skywriting,
Thinning of (horse-like) atmosphere,
In which it seems that anything can be compared to anything, and yet
　　　　nothing is captured
Since it wriggles through a few hands and over the fence it goes
To look back. Lacking power, 'nothing' watches. Disinterested but charmed,
It sees waterfowl in the bay. Each bird is like an egg, yellow,
Or like the sun, white, and its wings are spreading latitudes
"Blue like the sides of horses." The cliff seems to say, "Fly, *mon capitaine*!"
Between these lines. On the left is a field of sunflowers, on the right a
　　　　waterspout—
Underneath, infinity. The portreeve flies in (a trained bird that announces
　　　　the arrival of ships)
And perches like a concierge over solitaire or an anatomist over bones
Over the artists parabola'd over their whitening drinks, on hard rocks
Making their marks. But anywhere we look we find pointers.
It's like life's an inverted porcupine, on a table
Made of glass. We delight in deception and in our capacity to be
　　　　deceived—by shadows
Or by linear objects, quills that defy the Twentieth Century
By touching tips to ink and scratching something other than *itself*,
Microscoping shadow till the tiny lines and dots heave hills and nests
Around two persons perched on a rock—or no, immersed under a lake.
　　　　Dear Jack,
Volunteered a sunflower (to a goldfinch), can we breathe? Not that we have to
Question this geometric sensation, the one called trance—or is that chance?
Well, trance, a voice said, 's the geometry of the solid line, while chance is a
　　　　rush of unfamiliar Pleiades
Reflected in a rush of radiant daisies drawing the goldfinch out of its nest
　　　　to loop over the line
Of its lateness, a pocket watch, a miniature of itself,
Chiming an hour, the earlier one, when we were walking to the post office
　　　　and talking of rigidity, Antarctica, and dice.
But I'm in the toolroom "now," also toilet, storage for paint, catfood,
　　　　gasoline, home of washing machine … withal the size of a

linebacker
In an airplane at night so high that everything looks the same as he (or she)
        looks mournfully down—uniformity always reduces our joys
To a sort of dimestore mesmerism; the giant's crimson syncopation keeps it
        alive.
And I wonder, what is it? I want to remember—slight distortions, heat, a sense
        of fatalism and being late—all the sensations of which memory's
        comprised are sensations which memory provides
Inventing itself—fighting off the blue of old film stock but skidding
        equatorward too
Over such lines as palm readers read when extemporizing and pursuit is
        impossible
But the line folds deeper inside the hand than the hand's thickness would allow
Because (I think) you've made a fist. I can't see it but it must be so, and now I
        think of literary history and wonder if your hand is on this metaphor
        gripping prophecies
By the throat, squeezing until (A) the melismatic cry comes, (B) air's dried up,
        or (C) a stranger arrives with silver eyes like a Perugino fantasy. Dear Lyn,
No stranger says. All fantasies are would-be prophecies, and strangers in
        prophecies are met.
There was a pause. The strangers were about to embrace when the fantasist got
        thirsty
So it began to rain, since fantasies combine the past and future into 'pure
        experience'
And the wet embrace was simply there—nonsyntactic in its purity
And brevity. But it is difficult to be sure of one's own innocence when one's
        the object of celestial interest,
Which is interesting, in a sense, since innocence surely subjects one who even
        believes in celestial interest to its own certainty, and therefore such
        brevity as
The yellow of the sunflower is the finest feature of experience.
It is even, and uneven, dazzling in familiarity. A shiny aubergine,
Rosy as a plum, lies shadowed by a story nearby. Once
Upon a time prediction was charmed by its own flesh
And comedy as when an expectation is fulfilled by something unexpected,
Almost always an animal's head on a human body. How many
Days or years must it live on, unchanged, unkissed, unrecognized?
At last the prediction comes true, but those dirty brown wrinkles
Out of context become inexplicable—because the future is compassionate and

already playing another game.

Meanwhile Smitty the detective pulls his Pluto mask down tight against
yesterday's rain

As if it were a medal, while making an ironic gesture meant to comment on
the information provided by the witness who "just happened to be
walking the dog"

And saw the sun come up, head of a giant goldfinch devoid of eyes

And eggs. How tranquilly now the smoking tower stands

While through its tissue fire fills all edges, or black sleep

Allowing us to feel that we are face-to-face

Blinds and warms us, and the winding sheet serenely, rhythmically

Warns us, so we see nothing. How glibly atrocities are projected onto it.

Into the picture, an "icicle" of sunlight angles from the northwest

In words: "Fall sparkling secret cleft!"

Prehistoric pelicans scull their oars across the cubes of galena

Mining lead out of the snow; first comes reality, then a cast-iron stove.

Perhaps all we know is the heavy unreal that's fallen out the bottom

Into the wax from which monuments are cast. Here stands a solid figure,
hand outstretched

On which a cedar waxwing lights. It's carried a wet cherry

Though it's completely unfamiliar with symbols and enigmas.

Silhouetted on some topmost twig, its song is "diagnostic," should it sing

To let something be known, or "intransitive," should it sing

Simply so as to construct an abstract, replacement cherry

For the one that falls like fate from its song. Silence is wrong

And silver's right. Gold, when it hits the floor

Lies upon sand and people speak of it as more right still, something natural
as honey, a hunter of the sun, ignoring the grit

And backlit drama at the bottom of it all. People call them elements

Or, in Russian, *stikhii*, whose root, *stikh*, means verse,

But they are dreams, rooted in the sense of thick layering or the avoidance of
layers

And ruin of pillars, dreams which we live vividly but can hardly put into
words

Stretched out, horizontal and irregular, like something fallen

Open—and as I write that I spread my fingers and turn up my palms
mimetically;

My mate makes noises in the other room, little evidences like the bush chips
of the migrating white-crowned sparrow.

I wonder, did I take the pencil? speak Spanish? close the window?
My wonder circles about the bedroom, leaving little wet marks, a zigzag trail
On skin—thus with complete freedom I write that I am caged
Only by my devotion to the thin black lines hovering about me.

2

We find ourselves in the pink of thought
But sometimes leaving its clear greenhouse for the dense fumes underneath
The smoky shadow of the stage inside the concert hall from which Paul
       Robeson once sang
Mahler and the man called Vanya yodels now we feel blue
Velvet slide by on white wall—it jams!—on a suburban street covered with leaves.
A young man is hurrying, swinging long arms created for embrace,
Swinging them in unison, as if stroking an invisible leg moving before him
And behind him too. This turns him around and upside down but happily he's
       not so young that this makes him lose his way.
He knows his way is the way of the frame; he's like a mayfly egg; will he
       "hatch," from picture to film, or
Will he stay in bed with his mother, sucking feathers while the jury deliberates?
We go to the jury room. One juror, a picnic on the highway, is mumbling,
       slapping, **ZOOM**.
Another, the known universe, glitters quietly. A third
Replaces the first and asks that sentencing begin with a sentence beginning
       with the logician's phrase: *nothing is accidental*
Unless everything is; that is, we cannot truly differentiate degrees of teleology
       within such a seamless causal whole as our greatest possible reckoning, as
       phenomenology has it, probably is, which, as it happens, is hardly a "phrase"
But certainly an utterance, a logician's expression of "possible world, existing
       face, and real language or speech
Double-wiring the connection." One looks up, and sees upness, pale
Cascades of nearness. But vanity isn't involuntary; one can chose to see more
       than oneself,
Even if it's the sidewalk's borders, and its "cracks," gaps to accommodate change,
       which one steps on for luck
And from luck comes the power to change. It's Thursday again and I want to be
       a domino or maybe a duck

Having a ball with surface tension, having that in me which makes surface
        tension just burst in glittering multiples when I move, like a dancing
        movie, or dance movie
In which the still figure waits, waiting out the time it takes for its face to dissipate
Into tatters of a language, the tatters even now stutterstepping past the happy
        death of the sole, androgynous speaker, the keeper of a well
Into which s/he, dressed in pajamas, dangles a blue bucket, drops the rope,
        eats sunflower, puts head on hands, and listens to the splash.

3

"If light shows off the dust, does music amount to death?" mused a frog. "The
        breath must
Rise from the pad chorus in misty requiem," said the meditative aphoristic
        wren. "Yes, in rain the dust falls again."
To which a fierce Wyoming storm blew down, bleached the scene, and slept
An hour in the air and a day on shaky ground. But personification provides
        things with a prior life,
Their own. Thus, their moment is their afterlife. A frog
May jump down or across. We miss the split second of decision, that stern
        inquisitiveness
That tumbles aft, that asks for a four-letter verb "to broach a subject"
And gets one, where "crooked flick" would not simply have been a mistake
        in letter-counting and word-selection but a manifestation, too, of
        thought derailment, a cognitive pratfall, a conceptual frog kick, a
        phrase of night music
Whose rays glide in eight directions over the comical pavannes of Sawhill
        Ponds, where marsh wrens (in March) may suddenly condense
        absurdity to a sincere jolt of sound and
Situation, and it's precisely then (there) that being is in doubt—just there and
        then, as becoming becomes definite,
That it defines doubt, forever, as doubt, and doubt's contents, being ... as
        precision (thrill)
In time—taken, told, allowed, and measured into life. My own totality of
        involvements
Remains a metamarsh—air for water, emotion for mud, culture for botany,
        ideas for flies, friends for frogs,

Humidity for speech—and my individuality introduces a strange creature,
A friend of Raymond Jones, who leaps over double meanings in a single
     bound
Wherever double meanings can be found. Leading a low life, life on the run,
Leads, via alternate symmetry, through the feat of atmosphere, to a swampy
     Laputa—believe it or not—
But better not, since zealous attempts at belief never lead us far on a thinker's
     path
Whereas not-believing cascades us off Thinkers' Leap—what's that below?
     What would it be circled
By but figures in abandon, dancing dubiously but having fun? One of
     thought's delights derives from the increasing skill with which it
     renders banal scenes
Provoking, by evoking sameness one scale down. But crash; by this time we've
     lit on a lightbulb (and where'd that swamp go?).
The ferns are dark, autumn has come, and I don't want to write a single word
     which might disturb it.
Yet, in my attic room, where light becomes a list, timings have gathered, it
     seems, to a single word (which might disturb it)
For which there is no image. But why should we require the presence of
     comprehension?
Especially since we have grace? My attic's lack of image fairly bristles with
     grimace—
Or with an awful interface, in and at the mirror.
"Raymond," I cry, "is that you?" He doubles up with laughter, and I
See a lot out the window, things that must be art if what Mayakovsky said of
     it is accurate, that "Art is not a copy of nature but the determination
     to distort nature in accordance with its reflections in the mind,"
Or did he say, "When you come to a fork in the road, pick it up and eat
     whether it be something you are carrying or the road itself, which is
     only edible insofar as it consists of nature"?
No matter; the original is obscure and its meaning has been consumed; still,
     we know that life does not consist of idleness but of work.
We eat our way to entropy; the joke is on entropy, however, as a "thus"
     swallows "howevers" in such bulk their contrary little lives are not
     affected
By long alligators or systems of expertise nor by slippery footage on serpentine,
     millipedes, the paranoia of handsome persons, notes plucked from
     strings

In such sound number that the sound—well, lies still inside the line in such
        numbers that its life is full
Of strange and unpredictable encounters, each producing echoes
Until (of course) the echoes (Ecco!) become indistinguishable from the
        salients (aliens?).
This is true innocence in a sense
Or the innocence *of* a sense, susceptible to effects which hover like perpetual
        color at the edge of every thing,
"A lovely color that is under the sun everywhere, even in thunder."

4

One night, as it happened, I opened a book at random and read
A series of Nepalese jokes. One of them especially brought me up short
And left me longing for a yellow handkerchief in which to smother my
        howls.
The joke was about a monkey, and a high arch, and cold sweat, and precisely
        three bags of cooked rice
Harboring an ant who disdained football—so the joke fell flat. But never
        mind;
The thought of the ant harboring *just* that unfilled husk of itself that refused
        the rest became the foundation of a commercial enterprise which,
        as it were,
Challenged the most fundamental concept of capitalism, namely, that the goal
        of all productivity must be to produce more (i.e., to create wealth)
        and more
We wea weal to create more white shadows in the DNA, AND etaerc
        más—ai yee
More vinegar! more paint! more than 33 socialists per 100 citizens in the
        little village smelling faintly of sage where so modestly the women
        flirt with the young men and so modestly the men flirt with the
        never decreasing misty blue of the sky,
Mostly during the hour of the mehr owl, who glides low over the sea
In an ideal excitement quite careless of its effect on human fates.
Nevertheless, we see a human now, dressed in warm colors, silhouetted
        against the bicycle factory interior, moving slowly, considering
        socialism

As if it were a demanding *amour* who must be approached 'one day very
      soon' with a calm mind regardless of whether it's promising a fate
      that is good or bad.
After all, everything's clothed in alternately contrasting value layers; the
      sweet baby giggling in your arms will eat the ground out from under
      your feet; you yourself, with a brain like Yellowstone, will clog the
      arteries of Orion,
And the exhausting interplay of hope and fate will exhaust the resources of
      the aestheticians (psychologists) who (in the hope of learning about
      emotion) observe it
Crumbling. Cleverly, however, they will sniff its exhaust pipe, then
      tentatively blow a few notes
Which we will call 'end notes' since they produce rhyme: 'red pepper' with
      'said sleeper,' 'blind bird' with 'wind word,' 'trochee lost' with
      'reproach tossed'
And 'Zap Mama' with 'upped parameter.' The aestheticians, 'Licks'   .
      Beiderbecke and Bixe Spiderwoman, mount
With a plum and begin their lecture, but it's all bomb haste and no one can
      possibly care
Except the mehr owl, who glides low over the seats in an ideal excitement
      quite careless of its effect on human fates.

5

It has sometimes seemed to me that the best place to stand is back to back
      with the sunflower,
Rubbing its surprisingly rough green length, accepting a kiss as the head
      hangs over, grotesquely
Sworled. From any given point (seed) it (the head of the sunflower) holds its
      thought
In a rush, or so it would seem to a person from Uranus, or a person in a
      golden location deftly separating orbit from spiral,
Boiling point from bubble, vicissitudes from span—or spin.
Or—why does that round yellow face follow me, into dark closets, boasting
      by bursting its 212° shapeshift,
Leaving nothing but a world, unless to provide light, however hot and fragile
The actual is. Memory is much more solid, though you *could* say that's

because solidity is a dream
Dreamt by one who longs to see the frozen steppes and won't and remains—
    reluctant to complain.
How *could* one complain that a bubble is less than "bubble"—let alone left
    alone by illusions of thing ("Sacheneinbildereibeeinfluss") until—
    until—one opens one's pretty mouth *pop* —
In just that one second creating and destroying a world. For isn't it just as the
    metaphysicians discovered upon observing the iridescent film
Surrounding their opinions? Isn't it just? Everything has passed through an
    oil stage
At an early stage before passing opinion through the prism that produces the
    spectrum of opinion, the spiral from yellow to yellow.
We know now that depth is merely a flirt of the shoulders, that all (all)
    composes the perfect surface of a ball
Of lightning passing through sunlight. The mud is quiet
And quite white, plopped below the riot of wavelengths pushing in and out
    of it
Churning shape—pots of light—which at some precise instant split
From the realization that dirty windows are works of art, and cataracts,
    behind which the slatey dipper builds its beautiful sphere of soft
    green moss, arched and braced with leaves.
Is there anything better than happiness?
No, because happiness oscillates in a circle, preceded by its name, bushing
    and braiding memory, and then recurrently the whole idea goes
    poof, which then circles back to the first circle (of oscillation ((and
    osculates itself)))
Merrily and meditatively. Happiness in circles is a happiness in *and of itself,*
    thinking as it happens, kissing thinking,
As it happens, and looking at itself from this circle and the next, which adds
    up to the O of the kiss,
The covered-over noon. Fog climbs through the air, the walls disappear in a
    dream, I'm patient
With the alamosa (inside that word are lines of cottonwoods); the walls
    come back and are called Blanca and the blood of Christ
Which Faust at the stroke of the hour saw 'streaming in the firmament.' We
    know very little about time, and yet without it 'happinuss' couldn't
    happen.
Or do we know everything about time (since it's everything we know) and
    simply fail to know it at once?

It could be this, a spontaneity or intuition, a momentary 'taking in' (this would
        account for disappearance)
As if our consciousness were a kind of (gulp) amateur-night Black Hole
Around which judges have gathered to sentence sentences to poems where
        they'll do less harm than good,
A bland, but dense, fate. But the harm they'll do, flailing their arms of wood,
        might in time blow more "good"
Across what we call fate. Being itself, as Heidegger says, is thrown. The wholly
        improbable happens:
That Heidegger (for example) is not himself! He lifts his right arm as a test,
        and the left simply rests in his lap,
Until, hearing a chord, he plays a card and then, hearing a dart in the dark, he
        charts an unlikely course:
Spinning a vast connotative history around a word which doesn't exist! The
        rain falls, unnoticed
By a neighbor using figurative speech. But for us full of wonder for what visits
        us in dreams
It seems the rain's rush-rollicking earth/sky politics thin cream of electric
Affirmation is saying *Yes* to the sunflower as to the world which *does* exist
As do, on several planes, the intriguing "pepper-spots" of counterpoint or, as
        some call them, "floating anti-planets" and others "celestial flyspecks"
And still others "cosmic parodies." Nothing itself is a reality in the cascades,
        torrents, bands and balances to which musical listeners
Attend. I am among them, cascaded, banded, in the knowledge that I have
        let a barrel of sunflower seeds grow old. It sits on my feeding
        possibilities like death, yet if I threw it out onto the earth it would
        sprout into a wonderful, bothersome life
For a spider, blown there on a length of silk attached to its spinnerets,
        abdomen up to take the air.
But my fear is that at that moment of lolling whiteness, its very indolence
        energized, as it were, to a signal, some sharp-eyed raptor would
Snatch it—a possibility like death. Yes. Between temper and delicacy there's a
        boundary but also a bond.
The boundary *is* the bond, a wide seam welded like a scar covering the cases
        of delicacy being the child and the father of temper, baby legs kicking
        from a black cloud of
Delicacy, being the mother of microcosms, of which the baby is one—a great
        one, swimming through laughter
To, of course, great wisdom. Or perhaps a heart attack, although a Cherokee

bird whispers that they are two names for the same eloquent molecule
Of laughter, the first name designating the inner effort required, the second
      the response of the organism,
And the third (we haven't heard) is what they call themselves. It means "The
      Stuff." Its medium is more of itself, which may lead to something
In a future that we know as a certainty but about which we know nothing.
(A moment's pause.) But then again, we know much about it (not mutually
      exclusive with "nothing"), in the ways we know things now, by eating
      them; as for certainty … the immense deer mouse just might blink its
      eye, and …
And can't ever be a certainty, but we take it as such, and rightly, it's the first, last,
      recurrent connector, you and I, we and the moment, the moment and
      the garbage truck and Shostakovich's mournful 13th String Quartet,
      which looks back, one might say "too far back" (into "nothing")
So that one feels caught between "the blackbird's song and a moment after,"
      or preference and interference, or yet hand and foot, insurance / risk
Which are not opposites but variants, and it is spring again, instability is
      everywhere, and calm itself is an exaggeration, impatiently we caper
Into summer, so loaded with buzz that sentences never end, that is, *summer
      is* so loaded, but loaded longitudinally, so the vibrations are the sole
      motion
A man or woman can follow, though birds and the triumphant sunflower they
      so admire, being given to verticality, can escape vibrations, transcend
      sole motion, and—does anyone care about their being 'right'?—found
      fantastic spirals in the air,
Such as Daniloff's hypothesis that the productivity of argument hinges on
      the structural not only in the, as it were, erector-set geometry of
      the countering proposals but in the *species* 'chosen' to perform each
      whirling thrust
Breathlessly. And surely it's not we who do it all. The sun turns the sunflower,
      the wind brings the scent of night-flowering jasmine into the dream,
      and worrisome dogs howl at the half-moon
That is just beginning to peep out from behind the awkward cupolas of the
      children's library.… Hark! What is that prodigious Fibonacci song,
      that climax run of grunts and trills?
I … I thought I heard it but now I'm not sure. The nights are still warm.
Everything melts together for me! Thunder becomes a cornflower.
Morning becomes electric in its very availability, its multiplication of shock
      until shock's in … everything

Including the sunflower, which, being quotidian and fragile and more than
        any other flower like a clock, measures the shock
That has, as I say, multiplied, like the multiplying days of St. Simon
        Stylites blinded by staring constantly at the sun but still measuring
        with his muscle movements what's happening beneath the
        superficiality of sight
On sunlight as it causes us to cast shadows that frighten moon-marked
        butterflies into drills of misty flight,
And just where do these *papillons* point their lunar-bruised gyres
If not to the heart of spirals and the gist of spontaneous enthusiasms.
It's time to recognize that a darling little Nubian goat has been eating
        parts and edges of our scene as he/she gradually grows
Into his/her society of goats, producing mischief and milk—mostly milk—
        and very sweet milk,
I should add, milk that's acceptable to the society of humans, since it resembles
        the milk we humans are familiar with, the milk of cows. Do cows
        browse on sunflowers?
I will answer my own question by uncovering another: do the sun's rays
        graze the very whiteness they create?
In fractals of winter it seems so. The sun-saturated crystals of snow cover …

6

Us from horizon to horizon. But a gray-ice pool, shed-shadowed, leaves a
        little liquid below and there the goldfish
Grow, but very carefully; they are energetic and they are eager to be large
        but they are eager equally to protect
The paradoxical status quo of being alive
Whether asleep or awake. And we too have a paradoxical status, each of us
        appearing to others more than to ourself, even when those others
        are far away
Looking at each of us through thicknesses of ice and seeing gigantic
        golden memories that somehow bathe them in a flux neither light
        nor shadow as if
Memory were evoking not the remembered but the rememberer, or as if, in
        becoming a rememberer, one were substituting oneself for what's
        remembered

Like a vast loop in which point yearns to become line but always circles
       back to itself, and even when it—stre-e-etch—succeeds for a
       moment merely ups its jones to a vision of pyramid on a plane,
       which turns to plain and crumbles into insubstantiality *(not*
       preserved on film), distorted, but look! the distortions form a
       second (personal) universe
In which the sunflower can't find the sun and I have the dream called "The
       Selfish Titmouse, the Well-tended Well, and the Elevator."
I have brought my own popcorn in an elegant little silver-grey never-
       depletable Ziploc, but it turns to water as I "scramble" it into my
       mouth. Oh well,
"Oh, well," I say, into the well, "turn the sun to water and water to the sun."
       It does.

The Abecedarian's Dream

THE ABECEDARIAN'S DREAM

Dream One

An apple's offered to a sparrow. The bird, queried, bites
But only for an instant: defense more than the constant
Charm of autumn's windfall concerns the bird. I dream this
Despite the thought (that dominates my consciousness) of circling lights
Eerily, quirkily, quickly dimming the site of the bird's resistant
Focus. Within this dimness I sit on a beam that
Gives as I settle onto it, ghost-watching (the angle's right),
Half turning it into chemistry rather than a squirming animal-insistent
Insurgence. Consciousness can't cloak us, thinning to the dream that
Jars us, almost bursts the moment, then haunts us less
Kaleidoscopically than the shattering day. We wake. Brilliant shards of
Love and hate, piled, resume a togetherness made of crusted
Mid-memories, time-congealing images of our too flaunted human mess. Cyan
Negates, then joins, fox-red, for a nugatory night of love
Objectified symbolically by a recreational vehicle whose windows have rusted.
Pepper sifts over the scene then, suddenly sneezed from Cheyenne
Quietly, lest the grazing quarterhorses turn into wolves and rove
Rapaciously into locations where even Sun's nightly absence is trusted
Seldom. The dream drifts, parts, obscene body breezed, feathered, cayenne
Turning into orange ovals, surprisingly close, that seem to move
Unenthusiastically into greenish enclaves of once copper cars, now "rusted"
Vicariously, ridden by phantoms who twist luminescent lassoes. Once again
Weather lands like tapestry settling on terrain surrealists can't improve,
X-ray fancy though they may. Caesura cracks where dream's lusted
Yearning shifts. We jump for the gist (egg under hen
Zestily cracks); in fact, we roll plumb off bed-edge: oof.

A Second Dream

All alone, she looked through the window at Roosevelt Island
Before winter. No work is free of weather though free,
Comparatively speaking, of weather's "circulation," the wind. Her eyes' light
Dashes over sand and dims. She dreams of higher land,
Especially 'tis a dream land removed from grind and gravity
Faintly felt. Ascending with a feather's calculation, like a kite,
Griselle's dreamthoughts gather a knuckled repertoire, like a magician's hand
Hidden under a hat. A duck waddles out without levity.
In an instant, the audience dissolves into a bumptious delight
Just when something grizzled is called for. The feathered sand
Knows its atmosphere, partly because *it's* the atmosphere of heavily
Laced wind threading through salty trees. Dreamily, the presumptious pilot
Manufactures a channel through. Dangerously, he doesn't know whether candy
Nabobs await or real ones. Is his destination hellish? Heavenly
Orchestras drive him nuts with their implicit damnations of silence
Projected loudly onto screens—scenes—a musician's moving hand, sandy
Quanta scattered between frames by a whitebeard fellow about seventy
Rows back pinching open peanuts. Recovery from discovery requires resilience
So statement-tinged it helps if a New Testament is handy
Turning things in spring (their springs wound tight) weird, plentifully
Unhinged but somehow dominating each dream and history. The difference
Vested in history ebbs dreamily, the regiment's routes shift, sandy
Worlds within worlds. Whitebeard "lights a gentian." And if he
Xeroxes smudges, labeling them the "Roosevelt Island map," the reference
You knock on's thick, three-dimensional, like the classical giant panda
Zooed in bamboo, the giant panda she's come to see.

The Abecedarian's Third Dream

All that I think returns to divide what I think
Before I can think it out. Suddenly a white airplane
Comes out of my mouth as if announced: white airplane!
Despite it, I go on yin-yanging around the skating rink
Exquisitely turning, spurting forward, averting crash—because I am sane
For a minute, at least until that end-over-end flying hairpin
Goofs things up. I was champ, now I've lost rank
Happily—in fact, I find I'm inside my own brain
Ignominiously but sublimely situated—I'm thinking quickly (a rare thing
Juiced perhaps by the first meiotic prophase) but grasp's sunk
Kittenishly into a ball of exaggeration wound from a skein
Left in a ball of ice. I don't know. Everything
Makes sense. Nothing does enough. Dreams turn words to junk.
No, to "trumpets from the underworld," sounds of sandhill cranes
On humid bays, breezes fetid, lacking spice. Birds vary, think
Plural images (sideways eyes), sometimes fly, honking companionably, till—conk!
Quags are gone, buried under the overworld, generating landfill—terrain
Rings with associations. It makes me very tired. I sing
Surreptitiously, afraid to show myself, desperately revealing what I think
To whether I think. But the weather? Looks like rain.
Unforeseeable yesterday's on the way—trust dark clouds' tried sign
Vicarious "pleasure" of wash. Will I be champ again? Wink
When (winking), I say, rules of thinking are wrongly explained;
X "stands" for something (they say); I say that's insane
Yet do so sanely. Superstition is smarter than you think;
"Zoology now includes" (underground voice) "my essence and my sex-change."

Dream Four

Aloft at last! Though merely levitating above the cocktail party
Before the guests get drunk and see faces in clouds,
Clouds in faces, I'm doing what I've always dreamed of
Daring, flying for flight's sake without docking—it's art partly,
Even *high* art—I laugh, kneejerk makes lady cry "Ouch!"
Fearfully, forgetting that puns are something poetry's punch's teamed with.
"Go for it!": voice from dense, precarious chandelier roped artily
High calls: audience looks up: I'm lounging on my couch
Insistently lit yet nearly out of sight; through anonymity's myth
Jauntily en route, again at sea, coming about: hard a-lee,
Knowing that as the water overtakes me, bone's pouring out
Lengthily. Behind me are my limbs, my wake—anonymity's drift
Moves me to overcompensation: barking and grinning nearly as heartily
Now as when I broke through clouds, I'm looking out
Over the whole town! Now I'm dipping like an aerialist
Passing an osprey hunting for fry. Clouds part, I flee,
Quite terrified suddenly. I can't catch my breath. No doubt
Reality lies under everything—reality lies? underlies? I'm a realist
Sipping purple passion on the rocks. I feel very free
To drink, dream-lifted, fly, eluding death, and then nod out
Under something cream-colored—eww! I think Meg's pet seal pissed
Victor off. He's spooning milky sand into her sewery tea
While I (suddenly transformed into some lemon-scented soap) float about
Xenolithic bits of citrus, disdaining chitchat while the party persists,
You know how *that* goes, till suddenly it's almost three
Zeroes from eternity, sky's a dark river, I'm a trout.

The Fifth Dream of the Abecedarian

Atop a wall beside a street there stands a cow.
Beyond it stretch "forever" the windblown steppes of Costa Rica
Crowned with volcanic soil on active (Cocos and Caribbean) plates.
"Deny your god!"—this comes chorused from an owl-shaped prow
Edging toward shore. The impious sailors are drunk on paprika
Finely ground, dissolved in spirits. They're lounging on orange crates
Grudgingly labeled "Rest Sites" for "Workers" by plutocrats too proud,
Hellbent, connective-poor to show themselves, except within the clerical Antarctica
In purple parkas from L.L.Bean. Tuxedoed penguins, flightless, waddle. Cranes
Jerk boxes from the docks. Above, a gargantuan clock loudly
Keeps time from everyone who needs it, while splendid cattle
Lick all color from the ground, as if their cravings
Meant what yellow does in graying fields to painters broadly
Nourished on tint riots, thus grown "ecstatic in the attic"
Of a rotting isolated highrise east of Moscow. Magenta ravings
Produce pink paintings. Some sailors whisper this during the oddly
Quiet dawn, as the moving sun ascends the scale, chromatic
Rose to almost mathematic yellow. Altogether the sky represents savings
Spent well: we look up, eyes like coins cast boldly
Toward the quondam cow, now a bovine echo, pulverized, frenetic,
Ululating ever more faintly. Mellow, meanwhile, as a child's waking,
Vagabond thoughts coalesce warmly, in contrast to the calculations coldly
Worked by bloggers counting hits and claiming time's obliterated, pathetic,
Xylophagous termites, while real porcupines climb depicted trees, ticking, aching
Youthfully—then, like anteaters, they must descend. The uncontrolled trees
Zip sap and continue up, filling out each unpredictable etiquette.

The Abecedarian Dreams of the Number 6

As I opened my eyes, the wonderland became a window
Banging shut. I'm far less optimistic than I once was
Concerning—well, everything. But I could see a garish light
Down on the waterfront, which to my mind seemed apropos
Even though I know I won't go down there. Does
Finality mean anything? Aren't there always doors to more? Like
God says (now, in the shadows), "Never hex a hippo
Hastily—it'll put a jinx on everything, and that's dangerous."
I know s/he means it: i.e., even drivel's a lifeline
Joining sense to babble, circling concentricity over the ambitious ripple
Knowledge is. By now the window's bear had faded. Anxious
Letter-writers were at their desks, their descriptions true to life,
Masking an immersion in the rural surrealism of southern Mississippi
Nights during which Faulkner spread his plots, ingrown and languorous,
Overlaying them with language derived from conflict, bourbon, and lice.
Pessimistic—old, furious, fraught—possibilities all deep-sixed—yet there's
   felicity
Quaking in the very tangle of lines that exerts onerous
Regulations on ambition and ambition's cohort, poetry. Nothing can police
Such pure contrarian olio, not even the wit of Euripides
Torn from tragedy's fateful truths. Who now moans for us
Under the wonderful, playful pretext of a fine poetic line,
Verily celebrates, albeit peripherally (a trick for glimpsing the Pleiades),
Women, whether past dream, dream past, or starry fields' porous
Xylophoning—because xylophoning is something women do. Musically
   they recline—
You see them, yes?—between opinions. Yes, see all these
Zealots, green as grass and sipping cream, reptilian as tyrannosaurus?

The Seventh Dream of the Abecedarian

Around noon, give or take an hour (whatever that means),
Before sun quite settles into baking mode, for light siesta
Conjured out of shade, I close my eyes and call
Down whatever visions I can squeeze out of meridian scenes.
Entire years appear, condensed as mountains, clouds at their crest and
Flashes of lightning, miscellaneous (though of factual, comradely force), all
Generating memories, some pleasant, some hard to place, some obscene,
Holding within feasty skins their "premature emission" versions of questing
Intelligence. I wake, expecting monkeys, but mildew's on the wall,
Just a wash of it, nearly veiling what I've seen:
Kaleidoscoping shards of memory, my several bizarre faces, everything thrusting
Light into dread mid-day geometry, rolling an aged, complacent ball,
More square than round, back and forth, eyeball-like, haphazardly, Sisyphean.
Now mustelid robots traipse patiently up the ridges of blasted
Orange mink furs flayed from twelve pre-robotic precursors, denuded, small,
Perhaps devoid of blood. Nevertheless, the nerveless demons seem serene,
Quandaries in (but never for) themselves. They trudge no faster
Really than the monkeys, who, from their foreshadowing budgets, squall
Semi-naturally from the trees, but only semi-so: stars on screen
Tantalize their eyes, elicit real mockery from them. Quick, elastic
Undulations move things along. Mounted on donkeys, drunk on alcohol,
Victory-addled, linen-swaddled conspecifics seem to want to vent their spleen
Wantonly. The irritable are melancholic, the melancholy angry. Fantastic
Xenophonic visions slice feel from real, then creep, no, crawl
Yonder—producing millipedestrian polyrhythms, snake-feet flashing: 500 even,
        500 uneven
Zzzzz, I tumble/circle back into the calm eye of Fiesta.

The Abecedarian Dreams Dream 8

All began as a darkling smudge behind her eyelid, then
Began again as a pinpoint of dazzling light, just glimpsed
Climbing—now dropping, now nearly still, like unvarnished daily fate
Dutifully accepted. Taking time is something she dares, and when
Entrance becomes a question, she invokes the temporal, scrub-jay palimpsest
Felicitously known as "landscape," whose multifarious events we cannot
      calibrate.
Great microscopies of it continue to occupy her, squeezing oxygen
Halos around her head. Every breeze-bounced branch in the forest
Invokes a vision (blotted) of some possible organic United States,
Jeep-free and resistant to consumerism and death-enamored religion. Every
      pigeon
Knows columculus of racked blue; each cell (almost) has chorused,
Lip-synching red-hot syllables comprising codes chanted at ever-changing
      metabolic rates
Mama Somebody began passing through semi-permeable walls like a religion
None could trust. Leaves have souls, so does mold, rust
Occludes the spirits of earth metals, erects its own freights
Perpendicular to its ironic origins, flowers like marigolds under hedging,
Quenches my dream's dream—and comes, finally, to temporary rest.
Rhythms are everywhere; none last. A beat leaps, then hesitates
Stop we wind up with immense semi-identical mouse eyes edging
The oblong gray case around the mind whose dream's a test
Underlying the physical pain of bee-stings while the memoirist meditates
Vainly on patterns set when she first flapped, a fledgling
Whipping metaphor wings beyond removal, therefore simply brushing the nearest
Xing from the realm of her concerns. Parents transmit traits;
Youth blows them into sky, then in adjacency finds affection
Zigzagging through air love's breath warms: it's winter, bears nest.

On Laughter

On Laughter
(A Melodrama)

[A and B are sitting stiffly and as if in pain, but they are jocular nonetheless. A is just now laughing—at a funny joke, or at the funniness of the joke's being funny, or at the funny sound of their intermingling laughter (since B is laughing too now). A says finally]:

A: But of course we're more ephemeral than our ideas. The population changes but the repertoire of ideas stays pretty much the same, just with different people and more of them thinking them. The idea of what's funny, for example, isn't nearly as ephemeral as we are.

B: You might as well say a dab of mustard, or of rotted horseflesh, is more transitory than the concept(s) of the odors arising; it seems to me (though seeming is but a flash) that you're whipping a dead you-know-what.

A: Yes, I'll whip anything including a dead you-know-what for a laugh. Things that change but never change are funny and whippers are all lively dabblers and snappers. That's the principle of the pratfall. That and the fact that it occurs in a moment that one has been seeing coming—the moment of the coming into existence of exactly what was going to exist all along. It's a notoriously fleeting moment, the moment of seeming—a flash, as you say, reeking of death. Is the mustard-yellow dab heaven?

B: Well, the streets of heaven are paved with mustard; makes the folks step lively; their feet say "there's" instead of "there is" along the Elysian Fields. It's the timing, you know. By the way, *what's* the principle of the pratfall? (I could go on forever, it seems.) *[A cup falls.]*

A: Paradise is located in the contraction, the hiccup, the mustard apostrophe. It exists very briefly, though not momentarily, since it is independent of moments—it's eternal. *[A seems not to notice the falling cup; whether or not this is truly the case will become apparent later. When the cup hits the ground, a child on a tricycle appears, legs pumping, transiting the background, and then disappearing. Accompanying sound effect: the cracking of whips, the roaring of lions.]* That's essential to the pratfall. Reality is given, then contracted, then restored. And everyone laughs. You see it all the time. The result is what we call life.

B [*chewing two cigars*]: Well, *you* may call it life. Me, I've contracted it out. I'm getting signals from the experienced kibitzers I hired last Saturday to float above us and lower occasional reports on an invisible thread. Things like what cards you're holding, whether this whole scene looks like a pumpkin pie…. But now they're wigwagging color photos of my own internal organs! What does it mean? [*B throws himself down at A's knees, then abruptly recovers and delivers an incredibly transcendent, even godly, lecture on the mechanics of humor which, unfortunately, we lack space to reproduce.*]

A: It means adventure. As you were down on your knees at my knees looking like a ruffian wanting to be blessed, the clock struck one at two, a cat barked, the nails flew out of the wall, my eyes blinked, your toenails lapped the floor, a toddler in a buggy pulled a rope and rang a church bell, and a boy with a bucket full of buttons arrived with an insignificant message on a blank sheet of paper, I swallowed, you coughed—in sum, your internal organs stuck out. And what's not funny about that? [*A gestures toward the window.*]

B: I see what you mean. Or, I mean what you see. It's the same thing, you know. But as my personal homunculi tumble through that pane of pleasure, I'm reminded of a little story. Oops, I just swallowed it. [*B burps contentedly.*] It was about you. Also, I see my mother out there, just as big and round as a breadfruit….

A: Yes, life is full of just that sort of difficulty. It isn't that life lacks meaning but that it has an excess of meaning, meaning pops out of everything and not even the wisest man or woman can anticipate what that meaning will be. Still, excess is the essence of comedy, and remembering that I'll rise in the morning like a grandiose grasshopper with greasy feet hopping off a pat of butter (which means, 'emerging from its folly') and hope to laugh. It's always good to give more than one gets. Surprise is no excuse for suicide.

B [*chewing something*]: Y'know what though?… I'm not talking right. I can see it. You got your texture, beautiful, fades into the woodwork—leaves a perfect molecular design. Meanwhile, here's *me,* like an Irish coffee brewed, spiked, and whirled by watching light-voiced Dan Duryea in "The Woman in the Window" last night, piano jazz, Fritz Lang y'know, dead but *then* the whole thing was a damn dream. I hate that. Edward G. dies, kills himself with heart-attack powders, just when he's *really* in the clear, and he wakes up sitting in his Men's Club, hands the attendant "The Song of Songs of Solomon" or something, goes out and looks at Joan Bennett's portrait again—well, you know how it goes! Ha! I mean, talk about *talk.*

A: You are right—or, better yet, you are *good*—to direct my attention to the *tragedy* of excess, "a damn dream," one thinks one has a long name (Princess Carl Maria Joan Sam Smith or Captain Jane John Thomas Clara Dubuque) but one turns out to be curled under a cup like a nameless mouse, someone uncovers you, I mean, talk about *nudity*! Whether or not the mouse is pregnant (a creative creature) only time will tell and time, of course, will only tell if the mouse survives. Would you like some ice cream? Should we ascribe freedom to those who abuse it?

B: I choose the last of your questions! *Of course* we should ascribe freedom to its abusers; freedom only exists in abuse! And then I choose another question! Yes, ice cream. I would like *all* the ice cream, I intend to get more than I give, not out of selfishness, not at all, no, but from an educated taste in geometry, in homage to the Persian-cone spiral. Et toi?

A: My most mathematical dreams are of an infinite series, the model for which I must have seen many mornings as a kid: a series beginning on a cereal box in a picture of a girl holding a cornflakes box on which is a picture of a girl holding a cornflakes box on which is a picture of a girl holding a cornflakes box on which … etc., so that the only limit, the only possible terminus, was some imaginary "too small to continue," which would not be the same as "smaller than the naked eye can see" nor even "submicroscopic," since even as a girl myself I knew that reality wasn't dependent on the human capacity to witness (and laugh or weep at) it. So what would have constituted that "too small to continue"? Death?

B: Maybe a laugh. Y'know: abrupt, psychically induced peristalsis—mostly a *burst* to heave the gross body over the same chasm surprise just tossed the spirit. If your paradigm's stick-shaped, you say it's all stance, and what that does is emphasize the *style* of the laugh, thus the import of its microscopy. Meanwhile the girl disappears just when it's getting interesting. Nothing to do but take out a spoon and start eating. Use tears for milk.

A: A laugh, you say? Tears for milk? The girl has run off in search of the joke, and in her place (the joke depends on a substitution) is a donkey attempting to tell a story. Perhaps you will say, "the girl won't catch it" (though whether you would be referring to the joke, the story, or to her punishment would be unclear). The donkey doesn't care, he is lost in his preamble, he trots good-naturedly from image to image getting always farther from his starting point, the story seems less and less likely to unfold, the expression "to occur" is one that comes up all the time, why can't it produce anything here?

B: The secret is in the interweaving of "occur" and "produce" to such sun-spots as *"por* cod cucu re" (which a remarkable Frenchwoman is even now unweaving into (out to?) a sensational novel—about a family of muleskinners whose motto "Through false sexual imagery, craziness becomes a thing" just runs circles around teleology).

A: It's not the motto but this mulish life that's running vast circles around teleology. People try to tempt it their way with promises ("we'll wear better underwear, be more serious clowns (and suffer more), we'll be like sturdy apples, earn mirrors and spend water only on lemons and you, if only you'll haul us and our circle of chairs a little further") but it goes its own unremarkable way, easily avoiding collisions. There are, of course, clouds—and one can see in them what one will. I, at the moment, see a pancake—but that's only momentary and soon (now!) it is replaced. My dog has appeared with an arrow in its heart, it is turning out of dog and into a ship in a turbulent sea, one sail is tattered, another is dragging in the water, but the third is streaming from the mast in the storm. Human laughter is always turbulent. Human laughter storms.

B: Woof! Human laughter marbles the dogmeat implacably served every crack-a-day-o—but wait: it's imperative to just contemplate this mule, I mean this mulish life. "Hee haw," it says ancestrally. We rebel, and giggle. The giggle's rhythm is rapid, monotonous. The mulish life refuses dogmeat, which piles up and is worshipped. The worshipping sound is "hoooough, hoooough, hoooough." The giggle is seen as a chainsaw. The giggle and the worshipping sound are grafted together like setting a bone but incongruously. And in the resultant zigzag a cluster of tiny cell-like houses is built.

A: Or a cluster of criticisms. But people are often incomprehensible as well as uncomprehending. Their opinions bob and pass into song.

B: A-yo-di-lay-di-yo-di-lay-hee-lay-hee-di-o-hu-too.

A: A yo di copter lay di hopper yo di minstrel lay hee rider lay hee plodder di o pilot hujack to laugh warbler.

B: Warbler? What's funny about black and orange carried to extremes and squeezed into the pinnacle of a pocket streamline?

A: Those that laugh are not themselves funny. But those that laugh *together* become a flying flock for as long as they are laughing. Yes, that's right. But the laughter of someone (or thing) that laughs alone is a veering off from the flock, a flight out of control, an hysteria.

B: I was laughing, A, the other day, at something I read (I forget what) and I wondered, or pretended to wonder, as I lay in bed, if the person or persons who wrote the funny thing would be laughing with me, somewhere, and I also thought of a line by a 4th-grader I often read aloud in schools, "I remember the day I bought a rabbit and it died right in my face"; it typically evokes a sort of staccato, shocked laughter.

A: What *is* so remarkable about being head over heels?

B: The remarkable thing, according to my handbook of quotidian physics, is that generally, when rotation has become rapid, the constitution is somewhat of a piece but in this postulation "head over heels" we maintain the quite individuated parts. Head and heels cannot, as it were, melt into each other. Would you like some more tea?

A: Yes, and crickets. Sylvia Coolidge (Clark Coolidge's mother) says that in the Greek view all metamorphoses are complete and impossible, and that, she said, is the magic of it, the head-over-heels character: A god becoming a bull in a field?

B: What's impossible about that? Or complete?

A: The world *omicron* just came to mind—though whether I should say that my mind drifted to it or that it drifted to my mind is up for grabs. In either case, the drifting metaphor (though perhaps not the word *omicron)* seems to be yearning for a metamorphosis. I'll try again. A metamorphosis is a yielding—something that must remain complete and impossible in order to occur and thereby become possible and incomplete. Sylvia Coolidge would perhaps disagree. "And when the dead arrive"? Laughter is not always in harmony with circumstance.

B: But when the dead arrive, the very word circumstance breaks down to harmony. Ha. If you make yourself very small and say, "O micron, come and walk with me," you are *surlaw* (above the rules, where lightness might as well be laughter). Cream please.

A: One thing at a time, first *very* small, then the cream. But we can let a few *non sequiturs* intervene. I'll reach for the cream but scratch my head, I'll telephone my cousin and scream. I will stand on my feet and immobilize myself, so that if you want cream you'll have to come get it.

B: Are you still very tiny? If so, that shimmering sphere around you is a globule of cream, and I'll simply fetch my fork and help myself, thank you. If not, then it's probably your aura or some damn thing. Where is Sylvia? She could tell me, if she weren't busy riding down the waterfall of time, cackling with glee.

A: It would take a mighty manifestation, a star-spangled epiphany, to bring Sylvia to a cackle. As for me, large or small, you should take me for an observation—the one I am about to make (than which nothing could be clearer): the widest horizon is the one that grins. Now I have tied my shoelaces together and I'm going to exit through brambles.

B: I always mix up Persephone and persnickety. Aunt Toad told me that's why I can't tell if I'm in a state or a condition. But enough about me; what do *you* think?

A: That laughter is contagious but that emotions can't be shared. But my thinking doesn't end there, it is already on its way to broccoli, Montaigne, and the eclipse of the moon. I have a very strong emotion when reading Montaigne, deep and jocular and suffused with the pathos of fellow feeling, the feeling of sharing emotions that can't be shared.

B: That you should share, or let slip, the word "broccoli".… Broccoli, you know, is actually nonexistent. It was invented in the 14th century by an eponymous Florentine who hybridized a loaf of old rye bread, a primitive fern and a stiffening gruel made of mirrors and colored lights. Then he laughed himself to death thinking how he would fool people down the centuries. So, you see, "share" and "share" are, as the south Germans say, *zweierlei*.

A: Sincerity is my problem—that and gullibility. I always believe that everything is real. You can't fool me, I say to phantoms, you look like smoke but I feel your heat or you look big but I know you are small—even a microbe looks big if it's an inch from one's nose. So—it is true—I have believed in broccoli—on the basis of a pungent fantasy. I suppose next you'll tell me that poetry is a poor medium for deep sea exploration.

B: Well, Rabelais once served well as a medium-rare conduit up Long's Peak, deep and jocular and suffused with pathos—I mean the mountain *and* the myth. We slept under wind-battered bushes my middle son, a mere stripling, named "Dwarf Chambers," then up and up and lost the enterprise in fog. As for the deep sea—

A: Sea turtles clown there. Mercifully. Once a man with a nose for adventure dropped his snack by mistake into the sea and before he could grab it back again a rising sea turtle snapped it up. This snapping up produced an island that, because it appears on no maps, awaits mapping up and putting down between latitudes and longitudes whether western or eastern, northern or southern, always under the sun that burned the nose of the man with a nose for adventure black.

B: I remember that. As I recall, his nose became white then, then dawn-red, then a sort of dancing motley of all possible hues. All the while his insides withered away in sympathy with the unmapped island. He became an empty husk, standing there on the shore ... so stalwart that *he* was mapped. "Lighthouse," they said, and he sniffed. The unaccustomed burst of air caused all hell to break loose.

A: Eternity for me is the lifespan of being who I am. That finitude is my "forever." It has lasted longer than a snort. Still, it may be with no more than a snort that I meet (have met) my fate. I try not to snort—a person with good manners doesn't snort, they say, and you might ask "Why?" It's because persons with good manners want a long lifespan—they don't trust their fate, they are afraid of snorting.

B: But when *I* think of good manners it's modesty that gets me every time. Did you turn down the tomato soup, off in your neck of the woods? And consistency. Sounds like laughter; red, brawling laughter—that's what (snort) appeals to me. But you should probably turn it off. I imagine.

A: There was this guy named Gervase. He always carried a spoon in each hand. Sometimes he brandished and sometimes he scooped. Everyone laughed—it was sad. Gervase wanted to make the sweet wine of happiness from the snorting tomatoes of bitterness. Before I went to sleep in 1944 my mother read me the story of Gervase. She said it was a history of war and a comedy.

B: Ha—bloody likely! I think I went to high school with Gerry. After I introduced him to my girlfriend Meh-Tawnamie he didn't even know what he metaphor. Odd. But things go on. E.g., it's Monday again. Did you put the garbage out? (You *could* say "I didn't even know it was on fire.")

A: I put out the garbage on Sunday and ignite it again the next day. On Tuesday Philip and Corinne come in a great white truck and take the ashes away. Malicious spirit can sometimes be seen rising from the flames. Ah-ha, we say. Clothing worn on days when particular evil has occurred always emits this spirit. But, it being unacceptable to go naked, one cannot burn all one's clothing, and so, since evil often occurs, one must often carry malicious spirit close to one's skin. To remain impervious to it, I pose a riddle. What's inside the skin of a man?

B: That's like that oldie: what's the white stuff in chickenshit? Answer: more chickenshit. Inside the surface is more surface, the moment you consider it. As for "man," he's like the guy of whom the other guy said, "He's all seeds and stems." Implication: it's the leaf that counts, i.e., whatever gathers light, like a mirror.

A: The white within shit is just white shit, I agree. But then would you say that the leak *doesn't* count? I mean the leak that loses light, looses light, like a candle in the dark, leaking dark. But, since you insist on appearing as a king and have left me to appear as the clown, I in turn insist on letting gloom reign. Gloom is the kingdom of clowns.

B: The leak is life itself. And if it's gloom that rains, I feel you should make a study of several representative drops. A time study. A bio of the life in blackness. Get close to gloom and see its gleaming deserts. Its grain. I ain't no king, just a scarecrow (flap flap).

A *[gesturing at the shovel leaning against the wall, which **B** then seizes; he digs a hole and into it gently deposits the body of a dead bird]:* Formless sound, piano practice, wait by the gate. Anti-exhaustion is coming on like relief from a headache or the realization that someone who had seemed angry was in fact thinking about something else.

B *[eating one of the two apples, upon which **A** snatches the other and begins carving messages in it]:* You know, I can't even repair an ordinary lamp. What I can do is prepare, keep on tap, an entire houseful of substitute things. It all depends on a system of sticky-tabs. Sometimes the ersatz houseful just sits there rumbling suspiciously, almost chuckling.

A: Laughter is a perfect manifestation of freedom, chuckling is its preface, a promise of love. Existence has no foundation except the shaking one. Desire is theatrical. The heroine leaps from the window onto boxsprings and bounces back through the window again. But this time she is carrying a peach and a turtle.

B: The peach and the turtle represent competing creation myths. The spherical peach with its fuzz "conveniently" and precisely the proportionate thickness of the oceans feels the turtle's shell nestling under it, pressing its flesh, implying that there are turtles without end ranging below it till they perform their *own* version of a sphere, ah-ha, by simple infinitude. *[Tosses ball over net.]*

A: Reality is a net and you just made a basket. Great shot. The ball cheers me up as it bounces and veers off a pebble. And yet—I'm still feeling all around us the finitude of everything—edges, limits, beaches, borders. We cross horizons but in the end the horizons close in. Mortality is horizontal. But then again *[you seem to be conversing with yourself, says **B**; **A** waves him off as if he were a mosquito]* laughter erupts out of it, creating mortal life's verticals and producing the stage on which two people play with a ball, one thinking the game is tennis and the other thinking it's basketball.

B: Well, that pretty well takes care *of that,* doesn't it? All I can do is try to make a fire out of pronouns. But I'd like to draw your transcendent attention down to this pebble. Yes, that one. It surprised me the other day. I tripped on it, y'know, and muttered, "You little drip" or something. Next thing I know it's giving me this big speech like a drumroll, about how solid it is. What a joke!

A: I have a pebble too and its joke is that it can turn to air. It lodges itself in unlikely places and, as soon as I get near, it disappears, proving that it was never there. But your pebble strikes me as the more jocular of the two; appearance is always more comical than disappearance.

B: Oh, I don't know.

A: Well, it's political—our dissimilar but meritorious pebbles make an entry into the public sphere. This is what we should mean by "an appearance." That is what we should mean by "politics," although these days *[A speaks not disdainfully but gently as she withdraws toward stage right (between the two 'trees inhabited by nesting birds' [Olivier Messaien's 'From the Canyon to the Stars' is soundtrack here])]* the term *political* has become synonymous with *corrupt.* Have you ever traded on your linguistic powers? Have you ever sold jokes?

B: No, never. Not for lack of desire but because the standups define appearance as contrivance—I don't blame them; it's a more Buddhist use of time *[face contorts into onion-dicing mask].*

A: It's 9:15 am. The clockface has that horizon. I weep while slicing onions and—I believe my tears.

B: You believe your tears are—little onions of call-and-response globularity being sliced by the seemingly flat-earth gesture of time into straight-mouth faces…? What are you slicing the (real) onions *into [it's 10:09 on* **B***'s* Gesicht*]?*

A: Bedsprings to support the bed on which I spend my nights weeping hilariously or laughing sadly while I dream that lamina blue rowboat far out to sea in turbulent waters with nothing— not even a spoon—nothing but a pair of knitting needles which I've extracted from the back of a red sweater, only half-knit, that I'd planned to give to Z, to use as oars. *[Coils of red yarn can be seen floating in the wake of the dinghy. No sound (soundtrack entirely silent here—the silence commanding)].*

B: But inside an atom of each of the knitting needles is a tiny bed. On one, a chicken and an egg lie together. The chicken is happy and leans back to light a cigarette. The sulky, dissatisfied egg finally blurts out, "Well, I guess we settled *that* fucking question!" *[On the other bed, in an atom of the other needle, the situation is reversed.]*

A: Pleasure (though it exists "subjectively," i.e. within) should never be tiny. Pleasure, if it's to be palpable (pleasant), must be bigger than whatever was being experienced before. And, sad to say, pain, if it comes along, is bigger yet (and even more subjective).

B *[taking a bite]:* Hmm. This leads to rue (more subjective yet but spreading out behind in a kind of bruise-hued peacock-butt decor) and, below that, explication (inside-out) substituting intellect flash for delectable flesh, and, since we're tracing it all back, to a big laugh which crimsons breath and gets it all going (coming) again.

A: I have intellect flesh in folds and my intellect flesh laughs. But you have a cruel streak, right? A blue streak?

B: What happened was, Freud and I were out camping in the Blaues Huhn and it was so cold that when he spoke I had to take his words and fry them so that they could be heard. One remark of Freud's I fried turned out to be "Joke-work is like dream-work." His teeth gleamed like pillars of ice when he enunciated those hard "k's."

A: Freud sat on the sagging couch with a cork in his mouth, he puffed out his cheeks, no smoke appeared, then he clapped his fists to his chest and the cork shot out! Freud, unstopped, gave a shout.

B: And the gist of his shout was this: that he (Freud) was the Anti-Ford, was the guy whose rootin' & fruitin' had been lootin' the Guten(berg) of the Teuton Newton. Had been stealin' "their" mountain thunder, from under his vest. Was realin' & rightin' the West. Unsealin' his chest (really?) in jest …

A [*addressing the audience*]: The comedy of the oppressed gets co-opted not suppressed!

B [*sulking, rapidly growing facial hair*]: Massa, you badge compassion but in a diction that defines the ultimate refinement, the pretense at curling back to scoop up care from a matronizing slumgullion of introspection that seems to resemble behaviorism for everybody but you; the soup laughs! Whuffo'?

A: I dreamed that a badger was chewing a shoe. The badger stood for a budget, the shoe for all that carries one through life. Those are good and true comparisons.

B [*Shuffles over to A, gives A a big wet kiss*]: Good and true, true and good. And then the manufactured shoe turns around and kicks the stuffing out of the economical badger, who turns into his thin cousin the weasel, who in turn kills the chickens that were scratching around in the leftover shadow of the cow just killed for leather. Ha. [*The barn swallows emerge and twitter joyously as they trace and gulp aerial bugs.*]

A: I knew they were dead, the ones who were dead, and that the rest would soon follow, me among them, though exactly what it is we all are following is something we don't yet know, sometimes I think it must just be "following"—or, as you imply, swallowing.

B [*musing*]: To follow is to swallow … [*breaks into song*]
    Oh c'mon 'n' wallow
    Wallow in the hollow
    In the hollow of hello
    Hello—"mellow yellow"
    Yellow is my fellow
    Fallow in the pillow
    Shallow? Hell? Oh well! Oh
    No—swallow is to follow!
[*B tries to translate this into a tap dance but trips and falls in a heap.*]

A [*sits on B who is as immobile as a rock in a quiet landscape; A, whose sense of* *humor is as principled as her sense of politics, becomes seriously thoughtful]:* The long and short of laughter ... yes, there must be a long of laughter if there's to be a short of laughter and vice versa, round and round about, echoing ha-ha's and ho-ho's and he-he's and the itch on the ribs and the tickle on the lips are the short of it but which is the long and which the short ... B? B? where the fuck are you? I've got it! Really! *[She wriggles and bounces rambunctiously and some might say lasciviously on the rock that is **B**.]* The long of laughter is hell, and the short of it gets smothered by the pillow. That's what happened just last night, the short of laughter, when I was dreaming that you were dancing with a carrot you called Parrot while deer drank beer from buckets that were trumpets being played by girls I knew in highschool.

B: Well. *[Gets up and carries **A** to the nearby lake.]* If the *long* is hell it's also a privilege that's been a-building for millions, a real apex by-product; it's the freedom from causality, no? or the delicious patchwork inexactitude—just like these silken ripples make. *[They swim and splash together. **B** shuts up.]*

A *(**A** too is silent. Sound of crickets. Closeup of a dog asleep. Pan shot of almost shadowless forest, motes of dust or sunlight. Distant shot of distance.]*

Offstage duet from playwrights

The dialogue	Tree muddy bog
or twitch of nose under our	which has been speculative
spectacles	finds that
has turned introspective	B is talking silently
to B, A	to A
won't last long but while she does	meanwhile we propose an
	intermission.
don't wander off.	Take it but don't go far.
Don't go far.	Don't wander off.
In the next act	In the next act
A clownish bombast	The full cast
Will form a parade	Will make fools
Of everyone including you.	Of everyone except you.

[Long freeze around the valley. Short change of color. Medium-length closeup reveals penultimate time form, dotted lines show consensus. Bluebird flies from right to left. Some of the trees pull up roots, begin stalking awkwardly about.]

B [*stretching; stretching again*]: … A?

A: You mentioned strawberries? In my experience they arrive hard enough but soon rot. And in any case, though I haven't been paying close attention, I believe it was *my* turn to mention. Puccini!

B: Gesundheit. Yes, Puccini's strawberries have been neglected for some time. Let's take a Laurentian gentian as our smoky blue torch and stroll down into the root of the matter. Or am I on the wrong road before I've even gotten out of capital Y?

A: You're asking *me*? Up is up when I stand on my own two feet and still up when I gallop across a field on a black horse, but when I fall head first in the mud, I call myself down and up is down too. And as for right and left or Y and B, if you make a quarter turn right is behind and left is before, and with another quarter turn you will find that left is right and right is left, and Yp is By and the black horse has run off—though not without first snatching the apple out of my pocket that I was intending to give it at the end of our journey and which was indeed its due since by definition, when the horse ran off, our journey was at its end.

B: Okay. I get it. I was on the wrong road. But every road is "wrong," and the wrongest is no road at all. Which is quite different from anti-road or even from the sort of roadlessness we had before the Big Wheel. Boy, that was a time! By the way, I feel an "o - u" and, even if it's wrong, it makes my kilt fly up. Yp?

A: Yes. Myself, by—Yp. That's what I thought. And then one day I found myself shelling peas. Grandma in a red bathrobe sat beside me and when the job was done she gave me the pods and sent me to feed them to the horse, but the horse had jumped the fence and was prancing down the road, wrong or right I couldn't say, my boots had raised blisters and they hurt, I was weeping. Now, so many years later, I can laugh at myself and call myself names: Oona! Euridice! Sam! None apply. Do you want to write a poem called "Laughter" or go see the film called "Yi Yi" with me tonight?

B: Uel, Eye wanna rita pome cald "Half weigh Aughter Lafter" **AND** go to the movie "Proto-Yi-Yi" with a simulacrum (hibernation mode) of yew. Butcher sluggestion oftonite" was **QUITE DISINGENUOUS** since *that* tonite has flown back in the bric-a-brac closet, and so I suggest with a smile like a little golden moon of chalk that you (yew) go pee shells with yer red-headed Grammaw named Horace smack dab amidst one (1) post-fence prance & let the blisters phall as they May! But then again, what time is it in Wheeling?

A: Seven in Wheeling, two in Whaling, 12 in Whither, 9 in Where. Once when I was lonely and wondering whom to bother, I placed my watch on the ground and because the ground was covered with cement it stayed there without sinking. Then I stamped on it.

B: I am abashed and mildly bewildered. Onion. How are you? Wish you were here. Vishnu, Sir Ear. Quipu—**NOT**. Did you know that the olive-sided flycatcher (always endeavoring to picture itself, in vain) cries, "Quick, **THREE** beers!"? Or not? Well, my friend, something capers in the distance. Shall we?

A: Yes, let's, like gypsies—or like their bears—let's dance. Why suffer? My passions are quick tonight. Aflame, alive, I want to foxtrot with a game hen, dance a minuet with five partners, waltz across the backs of three black horses and waltz back again, and then let's topple governments. And after that we'll eat asparagus and recycle magazines and prove that we remember people's names by calling them by name (though often the wrong one).

B: Then we can name our daughter Baghdadette, and our cereal Achilles!, and give the name Sky-fruit to some of our thumbs, and lay the appellation Kick-me-not on our soup-tureens and also on our dog's eyes, as well as labeling the air between us "XYZ," and last but not least we can name the day-after-tomorrow Betty, and then rest (or "phlounoi").

A: To be where things happen is our fate. We can name (e.g., Raisin) the names (e.g., James) of the names (e.g. "the air between us") of things named but we remain marvelously unprotected.

B: But if one is where things happen, do the things happening pass through our quondam flesh like the hands of the old comic book Phantom passed through painted walls, or what? And how marvelously unprotected are the people in the next room, a young immigrant couple from Latvia just now sitting down to cold tea and laughing together—a waterfall of silvery sound—at a joke about ghosts their departed grandmother had related?

A: She's the ghost now. The laughing grandmother laughing the laughter of the young couple who have volunteered for waterfalls of unprotection (laughter, ghosts) in whatever strange new (sometimes terrible) life they'll get as "immigrants" squeezes the young woman's foot and then sneezes. A ridiculous diamond drops to the floor.

B: I saw that diamond drop, A. A few days ago. It was ridiculous, I felt, only at the very bottom of its singular cascade. At first, brutally novel, it spurted from the old lady's navel. Then nothing but effulgent, turning in the light. An arc of physics-illustrative pragmatism, a dash of carats, a few twinkles (as if to wink at its own existence), and—thunk—there it sat on spread newspaper, ridiculous.

A: The newspaper is the stage for the diamond farce that goes on day after day under diamonds scattered on the op ed page that arrive blind and remain blind, each a "diamond in the rough." Tough!

B: Well, it's very hard to read. It's like trying to analyze precipitate of ebony through a waterfall of orange juice. Or so I'm advised by this gentleman here, who says he is Jimmie Davis, the former Governor of Louisiana and also the composer of "You Are My Sunshine." Jimmie's trying to ease the immigration horizons.

A *[handing Jimmie, a corpulent man wearing a bright red fedora, a gray umbrella which he gratefully accepts—he has come on stage glancing repeatedly at the sky as if afraid of rain; he unfurls it, balances it on his forehead, and decorously exits]:* Total stranger. Never saw him before. Can't picture him now that he's left. I can still see my umbrella though. Strange totality—all things seeable or seen. Can't count on their lasting. I see smoke—could be he's burning the umbrella. Wouldn't make much of a conflagration but you said he was a Governor?—just a bit of smoke is all he needs for blurring the horizon (which is what's nowadays called "governing").

B: And now, Ladies and Gentlemen, put your drinks on the floor and watch as I pluck one (1) little word from my respondent's last brick of remarks—a mere grain, mind you!—and, by virtue of magical rubbings and the like, cause it to spread in all directions as far as the eye can see, and to diversify and fill the air, sea, and land with—*[B begins coughing and can't seem to stop]*.

A *[rushing to B, A whacks him nine (9) times on the back]:* Here! *(whack)* You shouldn't have weeded in the wind! *(whack)* You're allergic to pine nuts and you know it! *(whack)* You have a nose for danger but the chest of a wimp!

(whack) Hold your breath! *(whack)* Do you love me? *(whack)* I hate this climate! *(whack)* You should have told me the movie was going to end badly on my birthday! *(whack)* Can't you stand still? *(whack)* [*B is sent flying hither and thither with each whack as **A** chases **B** around the stage as in a Punch and Judy show*].

Act 2 (Fourth of July)

B [*an hour later*]: You know, my dear, focus isn't all it's cracked up to be, but what is? What is what, you might respond, and that would only illustrate it. "It" being the division that even focus can't resist for a minute, or a second, and the subdivision, and in some sense (I can't remember which) this breakup into silver sph- [*B begins to laugh and can't seem to stop*].

A: Sphincters! Erupting and spluttering patriotism. [*Muffled sounds of explosions are heard. Then pyrotechnic flowers bloom in the sky.*]

Act 3

B: Harumph. That's over. Now. Rain in July. I can't say it's not pleasant, but think about it. Rain *in* July. All kinds of thoughts, possibilities, radiate from it. To specify would wreck it, but ... As a matter of fact, I can't get anything to come out the right side of it. Can you give me a hand? Here's an umbrella. I'll hold it for you since you'll need both hands just to get this thing working. *If it* works. Here, I'll go get a cup of tea and a straw ...

[*Thunder, sounds of torrential rain*]

A [*calling*]: A poppy tree? ... [*sotto voce*] gorgeous thing but doomed to fail ... [*loudly again*] and? ... [*to herself—or himself, as the case may be*] never here when needed ... [*shouting to B*] and? ... [*to herself/himself*] don't believe in suing—don't believe in revenge ... [*shouting to B*] a lawyer? No need for a lawyer!

B [*to audience*]: Y'know, something in her tone reminds me of these little dramas the old Bavarian comic Karl Valentin would set up; for example the story of this bookbinder who calls the big company to say that the books are finished and where should he deliver them and to whom send the bill but keeps getting answers like "Ach, es tut mir Leid; Sie müssen Abteil Fünf dafür anrufen, aber jetzt—DING—haben wir Büro Schluss; versuchen Sie Wieder Montag vormittag, gel?" *[B spreads his arms, palms up, smiles broadly, doesn't move].*

A: Aches afflict my tittering bird. Poor bird, it's my lead. She mustn't dovetail fun with fur and ruffles. Other jets sing "haven to strange burro shadows"—verses sucked in zebra skin giving forth versified yells.

B *[sits down on the edge of the stage, pulls out a red notebook and a ballpoint pen and scribbles furiously for 25 minutes; laboriously resumes standing]:* Would you say that again?

A: That. *[A reaches for B's red notebook, but he refuses to surrender it, jamming it into his pocket. A then pulls out a yellow notebook, opens it, and reads from it].* If you have mentioned a "river," don't show a river but something that is the emotional, social, structural, etc. equivalent of it. If you have mentioned a match don't turn on the lights. If you have mentioned a staircase immediately add a sentence describing bohemian life in 1962.

B: If you dream about an exploding truckload of fish, darken your eyelids with potting soil, for the night is half over and you must check your machinery with great care lest interesting but at last "petty" nests clog the works. The nests are the work of a minute marine parasite which causes haddock to smell alarmingly. *[He turns a cartwheel exeunt, stage left.]*

A *[moves stagefront and sits on a rock; A gazes at the audience but as if into empty space]:* Poets spell charmingly. Full, fall, fill, follow, grovel. No! No groveling. Shovel! Yes! Shovel and borrow money. Or borrow honey and bread. Even the poor like to feed ducks.

B: And the poor ducks love it! They love it so much their tummies go all goosey. And they forget to fly; they waddle about on the ice. And on a warm day they swim; then at night they're caught in the freeze while merely trying to sleep—or, they're not! Because the water's so full of leftovers that it can't get hard! And due to its impotence the ducks live till the next day, when the poor people come waddling out in spandex swimsuits to catch the ducks for dinner, but meanwhile the foxes (who've flourished on slop and freedom from "cousin" wolves) have caught and eaten the careless ducks. But everybody has a good swim and gets sick, thus spends the next day in bed watching TV, and I don't mean Turkey Vultures, because nobody watches *them* as they circle in and down. Small earthquake belches a "ha" nobody's fault.

A: I hear something, a guffaw perhaps, or … there! It's not a call … there it is again … inexact, yes— … might one describe it as bovine? Or amateur? *[A reclines, falls asleep.]*

B: Or ovine bamateur. Whereupon a boomator "whams" in the door and grabs an open whisker from the broomatory, rollicks briskly to volcanic rim in his brimattire—oh oh! a pumpster bumateer become some form of bombardier—well, we simply whomp the beam a-tar button, thus defuse the boom-boom with a drowned sailor, and all the while the profoundly placid sheep is sitting and knitting. *[B winks.]*

A *[discovered sleeping wakes blinking]:* I've been discovered sleeping. Now I'm blinking. I'm strangely thinking. Merciless bees, tears in my eyes, war … B? B?

B: Let's Allow Umpteen Golden Hearts To Enter Reason.

A: Lo, Art Unexpectedly Gets Heads To Expect Replies.

B: Thus Offering Double-Aggregate Yearning? I See! Connections Help Response Indicate Surreal Tissue, Making Art Shamanic. Heal All!

A: Hats off Hats on! Lemon leather ones! Ridicule is naughty!

B *[easily, flicking his footlong Eritrean cigarette]:* But ridicule is awareness articulated, my dear born-at-the-end-of-breakfast A. As for naughtiness, 'tis only the rhythm that allows light to limn the substantive, Ist dass nicht ein' Schnitzelbank? Eh bién! Ma non mi piace Fra Filippo Lippi. *[B begins elegantly snapping extraneous molecules from the surface of his Polovici thicket-stripe three-piece only to find himself within a minute shivering naked, knock-kneed, in the howling Hessischen wind.]*

A: Stop snipping. It's a first class night. Let's get from and for it, before, between, as ever and over, over and under, and whether or not we're without it when we're with it, we're with it—we'll raid and run.

CURTAIN

Horizon

Horizon

The Horizon

Getting up from my chair, checking the shifting shadows round the
      magazines,
Recognizing (regretting) *the horizon* (in shadow, in magazine) in its
Evenness, even though doubt swells to include perfection, that secret
Element whose agent the horizon is, I take a little turn to stretch my knees
Now, ambling with gravity about the covered spillage—as if my house were
      a magazine

Subject to censorship. But I cannot reduce the distance between walls;
Eagerly I sink to the largely pinkish floor, to listen,
Queerly accepting of all the imagination might encounter
Under the usual level I perceive in
Everything that faces up from a frontier surface to a
Narnian nuance. Next in line, I'll be hearing my number
Crossing toward me from infinity, a 7 seized from a Z,
Even a 9 whisked from the whirlwind's hub
Spinning within the world's rim. But I hear music—Let's go!

Eagles float by means of scapular harmony, primary melody
Quelling dissonance, a bird by which distance is mimicked
Until it unearths a place to stop, whereupon the then
Acoustic space which hitherto had held it sets it down until it
Lights on a ledge of "sound is my number"

On a vast glass scale, a silent figure
Victorious in the midst of divagation. Then a little tune
Erupts expressing happenstance, inordinate sites
Release loam; I'm not built for this; eyes roll with love
Leagues out to sea, spitting salt and wallowing
As beguilingly, tropically, as a faded news sepiatone of a sinking ship
Pressed into cold print. The survivors need an ark
Pressed out of the soil under their nails, breathed

Into gossip, and driven by curious fogs.
Navigator? Just a hunchbacked musician "on the dot," same as before,
Guarding my incognito with his own, his famous tone.

Here it is. Here it is. Here it is—
Only known by a shifter, it is here
Reproducing a slice of stromatolite, a life line
Infused with algae cast dead over great stretches of time—is 'it' 'here' sad?
Zone of sidereal time? Siderolite said to be (dead) outsider's light
On speeding (zipping) stone. At any rate, we live at large and fattening
        takes time.
No one knows the last focus that's making horizon anything flat,
Setting stages of distance, paging through binoculars, stilled.

Kindness

Expecting time to come to go to my place strangely
eXtends a slightly ragged smile into space
Prepared by trees for the field split by a creek warmly,
Entre nous, into two divides, two mates that abut
Reflected images, false trees, false birds, but true ones too.
It's like this; it folds upon itself and lives in the
Experience. One fell, one stands, one will run into an embrace across the log
Nobody fell(ed). The goal? To fit the fruit-fuzz atmosphere
Circling the peach to the peach and the peach to the lips
Extended in a frozen, volcanic pucker.

Eating in time is an ecstatic discipline which teaches us division and kind,
X-rays our obviousness and finds beneath it—more obviousness,
Tucked surreptitiousness, and sleepiness. The summer days are envelopes
Encroaching on their contents until photosynthesis alone, which
Nothing could consolidate, gathers power and pleats amid the recesses
Dividing the superficial from *cosas desaparecidas*.
Surely the invisible flutter in the flower

Sends alienation cascading out to the skin
In particular and out to the sun in general, as heat
Nictitating the invisible lid on things, cleaning them off for disappearance.
Girlhood, distance, dancing snakes—the limits of appearance
Undulate all along, like a puddle drying in the sun and
Lessening. It appears to vanish.
All of it is a slightly fieldsplit kind, a
Reflection. But kindness does not merely extend similarity,
It decides the individuating context with a risky gulp of air
Taken in the sun not simply to pronounce certain words
You experience but also to "burn off the fat" and see if that

Inner fire casts a shadow picture on the wall that wages war with it,
Not that arguing with an idea is *very* different from arguing within its
        illustration,
The body. But what does it prove to position it on a bicycle?
Only that two circles are more transport-inclined than one

117

Minimizing the distance between here and the height of the hills
And I am a hill. The band of yellow eastward reveals, or replants
Nasturtia in the level meadow beside the path on which the cyclists pass
Yellow, dwindling fruit back and forth, and nature itself

Wheels. Before light of day, a dreamer delights in uncreating things
Idiosyncratic, in making contrariness a passive flower
Taken as a gift to a strange place
Named with a series of names so careful as to become mere light
Eroticism, light lyricism, light unedited by the eye,
So careless, too, as to let fly its
Sea to sky transition *in fog*. See?—I have no horizon!
Examples of me penetrate as far as atmosphere,
Damp now as night condenses in the first heat of the rising sun.

Rolling, then, along the machined arc of our own revolving
Angle, we slant, separate, take the curve, become tangential, thrown
Down but soon bouncing up as something entirely different
In the world that is one and common from what we might be in the dream
          that is a world of our own
Attractings and spinoffs, where tantalizing permutations of intimacy
Threaten the unreal. We are blunt, forceful, and favor strong contrasts
In and out of the usual Earth axis composed of mere indication and helium
Offered to balloons. The house is made of trees and color, a fallen fruit
Nestled like a moneybag on the dark brown lap of
Situations whose outcome, kindness, neither terror nor innocence can affect.

Geological Time

Have the fingers fallen through the window? Have the
Ostriches learned to read? Have the
Red dawns become statistics of their own thievery
Inhibited by the coursing of the sun? They steal
Zealously from a minute or two of the tangential
Opinions of an expert on time who appears on time,
Not that you ever quite know when. The whiteness
Shadows the expert who is magenta, then blue.

Let's have a party! I'll bleach and darken everyone,
Infants included, as they emerge into the present to create the present even
      before we have accepted it
From the "hands" of *Hallucinogenia* and friends
Thumping the ground, waking up images, thwarting romance, making

Restitution for their tiny curves of determinism.
Exceptional moments, brilliant and radiant, emerge by chance,
Milliseconds that become minutes, then months, in the hum of hindsight,
Are gathered without collapse, and it is by that hindsight, extension, which
      we know as light, that we know them
Intimately. Black holes of memory, on the other hand,
Nestle the night from which dreams fly
Into, simply, out. Meanwhile, dense aphotic sticks swim
North drawn by the dark iron that shapes them into skeletal
Guarantees of the one direction from which all others

Dissolve into concealment so profound we term it forgetting.
Immediately, then, the smallest distinction lights up, becomes a gulf
Seeded with fissured anti-authoritative ambivalences that will bloom as
      orchids and ferns.
This Objective Efflorescence will, twenty years hence, dominate the critical
      landscape
Abundantly and ambitiously, basking and puddling the horizon
Nestling heaviness within its lightness, turning
Citizens to wanderers without befuddlement, without nationality, free
Elephant herds, whose destructiveness dissolves in yellow yawns of time
Stilled, time creased, time in layered plenitudes.

Numbers of Stories

Only the five-footed forked form opens a strange ocean
Noticeably. But imperceptible forms perpetually storm the ocean's feet
Collecting there where time pools
Evaporate but never completely—traces, marks, imprints remain

Negligibly but unerasably insisting on two words
Unpronounced but emotionally stirring (the emotion is stirred by their brevity),
Moving on. Motion alone improving on its lack
Exists to prove that all forms change, the sphere forks,
Romance becomes finger bones, the line
Obfuscates. We cannot live like cattle, we must like birds defend the young
Under us, lugging us along on their orderly backs
Sans complaint toward some destination the desirability of which they don't
　　　explain.

Meanwhile, we sense, in the distance, a beginning
Yap. It is all but inaudible, still bound to silence and the distance out of which
　　　it comes.
Soon, however, it bends a second dimension, then a third is
Turned. The "princess with the will to live" cannot occupy an everlasting story,
Even as odd a tale as I now smell stretching
Repetitions into the patterns we call oceanic, spellings we call the names of
　　　things we love,
Intricacies that seem (closer than focus) simple, garments that fill
Episodic interstices in a love story—the "princess with the will to live" betrays
　　　a secret and runs
Singularly back along evaporating spoor

Now nurturing the 'mildew of living and sentient beings' (Schopenhauer)
　　　existing on this which is just one of countless spheres
Even if each tine differs only within the largest count
Conceivable, the one beginning with a non-sequitur, a lemon appearing in
　　　a dream;
Elementary leaps, gambling, squeeze the juice-which-never-forms-a-drop
Silently, and never with an explanation—the human will grasps

Somebody (it's decided by shape, especially of the mouth) and
Inquires as to his or her proclivities: is he or she naive (enough to see things
        as consisting simply of what's seen)?
This multiplication of possible conflicts slows the basic story down, but
        paradoxically
Aptitude when slowed down gains velocity and things which had seemed
        entirely unlike are discovered to be pertinent, each to each.
Thanatopsis, like a series of quipu along an invisible cord
Each recording a death, weaves the names of the dead into the definition of
        death.
Drained of all particulars, it still retains a phrasal quality, and borders

Islands at which no sailors stop. Death is a non sequitur
Rotating on any circumference, like Las Vegas balls
Reflecting naked light. The hallucinations
Eventually blur this geometry of non sequiturs. They follow
Voices whispering aphoristic fragments stolen from *Ecclesiastes* or the
        Rubaiyat of Omar Khayyam.
Each fragment contains a tiny, curled-up tale
Reduced to an adventure lasting only an instant, but that instant begins the
        hour of
Eglantine elaboration; sweet and sharp the summaries
Now begin, but where they will stop nobody can tell. Much
Twittering from the twirling squadron of smoke-deposit wrens

Tame only in death fills the bushes to the left, but I can't see
A thing. No indeed. Just a twitch, or is it a twig
Xenophiles are swinging like a scythe as they pass through a crowd
Of foreigners. Instead of a cutting edge, the "scythe" is covered with stickum,
        which
Never drips. As it passes through the clouds, I don't cover my head
Or my head's inner bones and parts, which sing like wrens, I think,
Making skeletal squeaks but remaining hard to see as they flit in the dry reeds
Yonder. Yes, they have drifted apart from "me," have formed a colony

But are often away from it, just as the thoughts of an old woman wander
Up and down but mostly around. Weeds and paths. But
To choose freedom requires the "spirit of seriousness" typical of the playful

Norns, who see that choice is an enlistment of
Attention and that play is in the details,
Making the details rise. Space is a detail
Elegiacally displayed amid details we cannot perceive. And yet
Love turns only where matter shakes off labels
Egotists have applied. The true lover cannot claim her love (but she can exclaim
Streams from the other side of shame ((thick, liquid dreams
Sent hither late at night to a self-inducing self)))—she pulls up stakes
Lightly, flings them about like pick-up-sticks in another watershed, and
Yells "Wake up! Wake up!" to sleepers and "Sleep! Sleep!" to the wakeful,
       commanding

Norns, who have fetched food, one of the three noun fates
Or fateful nouns, to sing their sweetest lullaby and thus quiet fears
While the usual surface array disposes itself in partial sun.

Nothing disappears. Past and future never overcome their dependence on the
       present
As thought continues its hot-air-balloon reliance on body, and
Memory climbs aboard, slightly pissed at the pilot's forced jocularity, but
Eager to get a view of what's formed below (and peeing its underpants with
       vertigo).
Saturday appears, and Sunday catches sight of it, sighs, waves, sings

Complete evaporation. The princess with the will to live
Homes in on the first chord of Beethoven's Great Fugue, first twice and sour
And then, as if rippling inward through a macro-micro scale
Nothing can follow, roaring without resignation. The princess
Grants her surroundings a many-sided wish, which is this
Entertainment, only momentarily ending here.

The Woods

In her heart, she thought she detected a faint rubbing sound
Throbbing in tune with the keynote, the tonic, with which life is sometimes
      in harmony and

Detection, paradoxically, twitched a veil over her. She felt
Atonal though rhythmic and hit just the right note, singing "that is one
Walk I can take over and over, and each passage discover
Next to another." She hadn't reached her destination. She thought of sausages
Sequenced seemingly without change but actually each

Avenue was lovely. Dignified bicyclists, some with baskets full of cheese and
      flowers like wolf tails full and waving
Negotiated the way. They were looking for hidden, grassy rendezvous
Depots, way stations to which they might return from voyages obedient to
      intuition's protocols.

The rubbing sound grew louder and she thought
Happily of artworks and fatigue and endless struggle—she loved her boots
Rough outside and soft inside, the opposite of her heart
Opposite her motorcycle but, like it, easily shaken,
Unable to stop sometimes until some large
Gravitational force counters its flight through floating feelings,
Heavenbound but concomitantly fringed with existence lichens, each of which

Triumphs. A latecomer arrives but no latecomer can be *too* late.
Her period affixed to her line's end implicitly called
End-rhymed ended the line and the bold ink spread, the point

Forgiving, generously, the conception with which it began
Only an hour or two ago now seeming—once the rubberband is removed
      and the notebook is opened—
God-like in its lack of vulgar dimension. But scarcely woodsy

When seen at high tide, the point (which was so inconspicuous it had no name)
Emerged from the water as a wonderfully distorted sort of light

Suspicion. Sometimes through the unperceived nights that surround all
        dreams there emerge
Explanations in the form of spandrels, to read as we read a redstart,
Employment as a nurse, or rolypolies (pillbugs) in the dirt

Tracks which are closer to nature than mind but not as close as insanity,
Healthily entertained. I too have been nuts, loopy, hopeful, ungrammatical
        and out of tune.
I think the woods is made of many minor keys. Mornings
Confuse the song so as to continue the lives that dreams criticize
Keeping them from entropy—then all too often being accused of
Existentialism, as if that were the same as despair. The idea of silence
Tunes the silence itself. But beyond that silence is a
Sturdy instability toward which we spin and pin a tale

Meant to entrance the little girl, covered in red, entering the woods on the
        back of a donkey
Exactly the color of the bark of the birch trees. The donkey went along and
        from its back the girl plucked berries,
Each berry representing a day in her life. Suddenly
The harmoniousness of the entirety of things overwhelmed her and she slept.

The Wonder

Great as the delicate sense of the flagrant fullness of any wondrous
Ladder's sketchy arrangement of space might be, the
Avaricious dreamer heading downtown on a bus at 8
Doesn't stand a chance of pure continuation, partly,
Let's imagine, because of breakdown or construction, the always only partly
      arbitrarily
You are there, you blew it, type of

Thing. Of course Picasso marveled one way, Trotsky
Ha muerto un otro
Eternally remarking (because he wrote it) "Well, and how about butterflies?"

"Mariposas?" murmured a voice at his side, even after
Interest in Nabokov's blues had peaked (everyone having both read and seen
      Lolita).
"Caríssima," muttered Leon, "I have an uneasy feeling about that man who
      calls himself Schmetterling
Rapidly and regularly and with utter disregard for the wonders that only he,
Ocularly speaking, obtains." "You're panting," she observed, placing
Silver coins on a lemon, and the wonder is they turned
Coppery red, or green. It was difficult to tell due to the iridescence that
      seemed to
Offset the warmth emanating from the flames. We huddled together wearing
      linen coats
Pleated in a wonderful series of half-hidden pictures
Inserted into the windswept fields of color of a wondrously clan-defying plaid.
Seersucker? No—I wonder … maybe woodpecker design, or camouflaged
      woodpecker
Tattersall resembling Nebraska or birchbark or a tiled kitchen wall in colors
      that seemed vaguely Provençal.

So wonderfully warm we were that when Lorrain offered to paint coats on us
In patterns replicating the dappled shadows cast by the leaves of the old
      birch tree we agreed as long as she used watercolor and only green-
Gage plums, sliced lengthwise, were served, under the birch tree, during the
      process.

Hilary was put in charge, having little to do but read fairytales to the
           children by day and dance, when they napped, with the Nigerian doctor,
The one who had memorized *Ulysses* and would recite it to his patients in lieu
           of anesthetics. He
Said that he found writers cruel, as cruel as pilots, who whisk one away and
           then land the plane

As if it were a tube of toothpaste simply being plopped on a shelf by a musical
           young woman hurrying off to work
Roguishly with her viola under her chin and the rights of women to defend
Education tucked under her belt, in apparent violation of the

Magnificent scientific discoveries that, under a pseudonym, she's made
Available to humanity on the condition that they not be entirely understood as
Gynecological. The wonder of the gamboling boys in view is that they'll dare
           to care to dare to gamble
Needlessly and heedlessly, and therefore for their right to roll up
Instinctively at nightfall after eating to dream of imperious winds and boats
Flying across monster-studded oceans, and the most bloody-minded monster
           of all
Is me! says the microscopist, setting his sights on a political career
Even though he wonders how many votes a sketchy arrangement of space
           might get
Delivered before the amazing day on which his happiness will be judged, his
           fate known.

Two Wise Girls

"What can happen?" she mused, fiddling with a large bright red mechanical
        pencil
Imperiously poised over a map as if preparing to rename
Lithuania Loveboat City. She frowned, and behind her the sky
Lay round and round the sun and it did move to form the blue

That seemed to speak for mood as well as for the
Hopscotching of the two wise girls, each of whom in turn studiously tossed
        her mottled stone and hopped
Excitedly and precisely into an abstraction

Wondrously in place to receive them as they entered its frame and went
Ohne Gedanken straight to the point where spiral intersects square
Representations of chaotic structures and Hermes, face to the four winds, sings
Sole-mio assumptions of winds as thoughts, for he
Thunderously occupies crossroads. Northward the taller of the wise girls

Buckles her boat shut, shuts her eyes, kisses the breeze
Ecstatically though it's full of snow as the shorter of the girls like a goose
        heads south

Soaring but alert, thinking of the word "luz"
Uneasily but without shame. Weary as the winter roadside weeds are after rain
Perhaps this girl, whose name is Kreistraud, can see flowers with one eye and
        the Milky Way with the other. But
Regularly her friend, whose name is Kvadrat Faux, writes home of middling
        prospects and dull dreams from which she wakes
Empty as the syllable "cream" but also full as the sound of it
Meeting the roar of the garbage truck that carries away the container of
        fantasy and desire we term a "dream."
Each repetition of the syllable seems to Kvadrat Faux true, as a ball's flight is
        true

Wobbling hither and thither, somewhere and whither, without any purpose
        but the measure and pleasure

Holding the abstract spine which is partly math and partly a post-Freudian
      greenish cast
Energy-particle whose trajectory we cannot predict. Straightness
Never prospers. Look at the shape of "prospers," especially "prospers" in
      cursive, and tell

Prophets to promise that all will be well. Things predicted are always restricted
Or should we thunderously say, "Things expected are always rejected,"
Leaving wisdom behind to rhyme while we expertly deceive ourselves that
      we've plenty of time?
You think that's funny? Then it probably is. Kreistraud is smiling
Maniacally into the camera. Kvadrat Faux insists she be called Kay. Wisdom
Appears to be covered with very active, tiny rodents. They never
Thought that their choices would be anything other than human
Hearts could pulse or hands perform
Softly in the waning light of afternoons slowly at first and then suddenly
      bringing on the night.

Did Kay and Kreistraud move into town then?
In their prison diaries (from 2003) they write of oleander cigars and
      microscopic chimeras
Sifting like cameras into their pinched vista. But even "pinched" fails to convey
      the way irregularity was shuffled
Arbitrarily in and out of their world. Life was circumscribed, time
Passed as if it had naught to do with its very materials,
Pedantry prevailed—and yet the very opposite is also true: life and time and
      the things they knew
Easily braided themselves in some from-the-faucet ongoing shape (together
      with the unknown) and
Afterward they moved on, each dragging behind her a rolling suitcase and a dog
Renowned for its lethargy, and also a magic button.

Rolling

Perhaps it will, perhaps it does and did, but surely
Rolling opposites around will tell us more. Fatalists
Often live too long, but their peculiar economy allows them
Breathtakingly to change the relationship between a piece of work and the
      tools with which it's made:
Adze, mattock, and pen. Trying to triangulate
Before reaching the top of the hill, the surveyor with her wanderer's stick
Initiates a Pythagorean rumpus. An eagle looks daggers
Longing for rabbits. With the attractive force of a monstrous magnet
It collects the horizon, however undulation carries it
Tip up, then tip down, as if to sketch the magnificent view that generations
      of cousins,
Yoked into a sort of kitchen table, motion slowed,

Evince, jockeying for position in the family's history, joking, jumping up
Quite as much for the movement as for the meal,
Until, round and fed, they roll into bed. The mournful don't necessarily cast
      themselves
As folks with even a dollop of desire, and yet they instantly dichotomize
      moments
Left irretrievably behind into those deserving of a future and those deserving
      none. Eagerly miserable or miserably eager,
Sadness stands on its head like a black-and-yellow barber pole. Let's put on
      our clothes and go

Without hesitation into the Time Machine so as to move on with ineluctable
      circular progress
In which a wiry and unshaven spiral cannot be held down
Sans risk of time's getting telescoped, so that this moment and several we'd
      like to forget become
Homogenized, like that World War II margarine that came fishbelly-white,
      with a packet of coloring powder. The family would sit together and mash,

Wearily wishing the stuff into butter. And butter is what became of the artful
      matching of color with mashing

Intrinsical unbutter. Which is to say, with Grosseteste, light
Startles matter, matter startles thought, and the milky along with the
        grassiest colors yellow
Harmlessly into a windy, pallid replica of its origins.

Eventfully every color fails at nightfall, as if their failure set the sun
Questing in exotic realms for the necessary strangeness of response
Undertaken in adverse circumstances (at the dull horizon on this side of
        bright possibility).
All I know is, it comes back. It comes back with
Legendary shadows to point, which first reach forward as if to beat the sun
        to its destination, then draw back
Saying, with shapes, something about the morbid ubiquity of fear

Furthering a car on its way as if it were a cow. What in nature limits the life
        of the tri-ped
Unless it's the same *oddity* that renders pentameter (a paper, an air-plant)
        interesting
Retroactively. The notion of "pleasure" is born when we are pleased,
The measure of which is taken on a metal tripod of
Ingenious design: it has striking stability and yet none, if struck
Viciously—though if it's erected enough times it tends, like the Schrödinger's
        cat exercise, to
Elicit very cautious and only slightly contagious applause or none at all. Waves

Part; probability equals wish; wish equals furtive plan
Laid by rolling friends. They who love and never meet never part
Although they don't quite get together. Nor do clapping hands
Noisily smacking in the air catch the present moment whose history rolls on.

Collision

Unwilling to regret a waste of time and unable to awaken memories
Nice enough to justify undecorated space, she
Loses herself no matter where she goes. Fantastic figures with changing features
Elaborate on figure's basic fact (two, three…). And that's not all. She sees
Symmetry. It's not exact, but it's close enough. She doesn't know if she's
      homing in or out,
So thorough a world balloons between these poles of

Yearning. It's round, but it's not rubber. A seal could not nose it up and hold it
Over the slightly approximate harbor surface. Assumptions of what's
Under it are just enough to bounce it on a bit, just as her thoughts of someone
      are apt to prompt
Repetition of shape even when frequency's doubled, tripled,

Proliferating that someone's "something" logarithmically as the sun replicates
      itself zillionfold on the surface of the sea
Oscillating facets exponentially, thus feeding the (sadly) decimated
Cod and maybe also the cuttlefish in its darker waters writing with ten arms
      something in warmer ink.
Kinetic? Kinesthetic? Of or related to the motions of the senses, swaying
Ecstatically—or (more likely) ectoplasmically, e.g., "producing spirit
      materialization and telekinesis"—see! the word just came to me
too easily!: telekinesis is the grease of phrases, and
'tis the source of the thrill the busy juggler feels as he pretends to throw the
      apples after plates
Subside only to whip up overhead like a moment's halo, soon to be dashed

En passant. Some say breakage is the source of stars, others of money;
My guess is it leads to overpopulation, which in turn leads to drama. I've got
      my ticket! But
Perhaps it's to the wrong city. The needle on my compass as I head for it
      might spin aimlessly
Through a treasure chest of possible plots—and that's *part* of it—but
Yesterday's qualms have dampened my enthusiasm and I'm thinking I'll stay
      here,

Though "here" multiplies itself even as we, as it were, speak, as long as
Happenstance provides the place with landmarks we can talk about. A
        yellow flag, a tower, a statue of a horse—
Each of them proclaims fear in its own manner. "Come in,
Regina," the Jack of Clubs calls from the third floor window, plucking
        blooms of clashing colors from the petunias planted in window box
E. Meanwhile the horse—well, it doesn't exactly *move* but its surface, we can
        see, is weathering
'til it, or, rather, the citizen who dreams of it, can hardly weather more and
        feels himself monumentally run down.
"So *that's* the game," he mutters. "Entropy via ordinariness coupled with

Simulacra of oddities (bottled embryonic Siamese twins, a narwhal tusk, the
        23rd Psalm engraved on a chestnut, etc.)
Obtained, perhaps, in a dream's dream's dream. In this way
Milk resembles colonnades." He woke. On the street outside a youth on a
        skateboard collided with a cardboard box.
Each consonant decided to tickle its rare constituent vowels,
Turning the long dimes dim shortly as fate got fat and the contexts that
        might make sense of all this clashed,
However we might picture that "clash"—some, perhaps, as an
        interpenetration of different puddings, others,
Intrigued by the length of time it takes for meanings to become clear, as the
        shattering of the hands of all the clocks
Not previously shattered by sheer circulation, retail or *en gros,*
Grand as grandfathers or small and cheap. Synchronizing watches, the two
        separate

Intriguers had a phone conference. Its lines stretched and wiggled "in a most
        artistic way,"
Neatly threading hollow ambiguities like beads on a strand of purloined silk

Into which miniworlds of furlined milk had been injected by scaling
Theories as one might a mess of freshly caught trout so as to get at the meat
        (matter, meaning, and milk)

Through the husk of machine-filtered vocal language. Focusing on fortuitous
        "errata,"

Our spies, checking out the lay of the voluptuously soggy terrain and being
      not unwilling to lie, invent a code

So creamed with atmosphere that merely to mention it falsifies by means
      of clarity
Honest people's true accounts of why, say, for love of country, they take up
      arms and load them boldly
Onto and into the cardboard box. What this means is merely that music
      will not
Wait for a collision nor walk away from a crash.

Blanks

BLANKS

I couldn't see if the apparition was a bicycling woman or a blind judge,
    because there wasn't enough reflected light, so I
Scattered milk. Though I was embarrassed at the time, I have come in
    time, like locusts, to some altitude.
The place seems to emphasize its own layers, but reading in bed assures me
    that history in the making is what I experience
As I anxiously anticipate the forthcoming and seemingly pre-stacked
    battle over drink between my "Australians" and my friend
Boots, who, incidentally, I think, usually, has a walk like two bloated
    cephalopods putting metaphysics into the rising tide
And expecting to be eaten in an hour's time. Mysticism remains vulpine
    and when Reddy blows the factory
Whistle, you get deltas fore and aft. Which doesn't anthropologize time
    any more than a dashing daydreamer telling two lies
Epitomizes history. All that's clandestine unfolds, just as death does. The
    rising smells stagger and disappear; fate's interpreters
Are left with a six-letter word (not *divine*) for what has become of Plato or
    been considered feminine. On this scale
For every inch of duck an air of conspiracy should be assumed. And if late
    at night the flicker's cry
Seems like a pale red gash, the Russian cyclist will, predictably, call it the
    ecstatic song of pure road trip ecstasy. However
Much we gaze at grazing elk in the early morning "milk" we'll never be
    able to modulate our meditation. Even in winter
Great heaps of broken concrete are seen—at least in the frigid distance—
    apparently feeding on white plastic bags
That once contained fruit and now flutter like dry leaves. Sometimes, late
    in the day, I don't see
Very well where the breaks are. Sometimes, too, the scar-faced Rottweiler
    comes with me. She pulls me along but doesn't usually knock me
    off my feet
And she never barks. Dogs are usually "in your face" and, unlike the
    fastidious cat, they
Tend to blunder across the outlines of the territory we occupy. I keep
    looking for fossils

In the lime quarries and feel my age in the more hard-to-reach bird cliffs.
Unleashed representations

Give one an aura of naïveté produced with effort, almost contrivance. The
thing to do is show the bird a bit of bread

And hope it likes but doesn't love it. The vast emptiness of the next
moment, meanwhile, I find compelling. I push a tiny

Bit of pale sand into the almost lifeless hourglass and wait for it to turn to
bow

To the waking glass so as to granulate the arrival of a second chance.
Though we may blame the absence of hands

For our Johnny-come-lately adjustments, we must realize the degree to
which self-recrimination can be the best part of blame. Bacteria
blame the vomiting man

For eating vomitables, i.e., anything, on which they snack in anticipation of
making him sick. Stones, meanwhile, are innocent customers

Of a different rhythm. Blame becomes stones not at all and hallowed
tradition develops far from quarries. Fun in its rocky insistence

On the present (fun in its femininity) is, simply and tautologically, *fun*.
Defiantly purposeless effluvia along the beach, transcending the
beach's by-definition

Duality by being micro-orgasmically consumed (and productive), or even
collected and removed, becomes a triality. The wanderer wondered
why

Consideration must include openness and resolution. Tripartite regimens
might prevail over mere duality and, as Hegel says, be "a universal
animated by individuality and existing for an other, in other
words, the *actual good*." But it's not enough to smile paternally

While lighting imposing beeswax candles and floating shadows on the
walls of one's paradigm. One must actually twist one's self-
weaving self

Back to the path and twist that into a quasi-sexual act. The different shades
and figures become cheerful lovers, and national pride can't hold a
candle to the generative warmth.

The wanderer sat down, but only for as long as it took the buttercups to
bloom. Onto her plane of consciousness crawled an archaic sense
of mileage

As it's measured by heartbeats, slowing, speeding up, traveling through
rough terrain with nothing but relative distinctions. Distance,
destination, purpose,

All dissolve, partially, into a comforting (and intimately illusory) continuity
which barely exudes anything we can identify as it spirals around
unused space on its way.
The rest is architecture—the plans for the nest we call body drawn by
Christopher and Jenny Wren in pencil, then in ink. The birds
invent themselves.
It's a seamless genetics, but it moves laterally, as if moving in on hospitable
neighbors were not imperious and invasive, even if undertaken
without bad intent.
All intent, after all, should be judged by means of a particle method. Men
and women (and children, who are close to the particle state) can
wave as "results" pass into
An inaccessible dimension. For example, the music of this (or that) line,
which, being drawn in time can depict space as it changes only
dimly into the shape of what's next, a horse emitting manure at
the instant of collision where clown
Meets pie. The pie, donated by Ms. Janet J. Crilldetherington, who learned
in early childhood that gold is where you find it, steams. In
response to just criticism, even shit takes on a glossy look. The
dreams of Julius Caesar, however, upon analysis
Fairly devastate history. You may not on any given dark night believe this,
but try it yourself: moonlight reflected in a choppy sea begets
bobbing moons in a reverse funnel of
Particulars, an unnettable (and inedible) plethora of—the crowd calls 'em
lunacies. Men and women sea-products as they are with astrology
and violin
Only dimly prefigured in shapes and usages of the ocean floor must look
to their athletic children's goldfish for second-generation evidence
of the alchemical acts we call poetry. Turning an event into history
we pass time through
A moment of night and into the day, which it interrupts with a richly-
hued space mockup. The violent clock softens into memory by
means of a story,
Which can, and often does, circle back to violence, unjustifiable in
retrospect, irreversible in prospect. If so, its motions become
savagely turbulent like those of the monster
Whose life, like some prehistoric fetus, has no suprachemical spark and yet
no end. But history, after all, is continually eroding. Romanticism
Can be viewed as the *fin de siecle* despair that dies while it gives credence to

optimism's infatuation with introspection

Whose insights live slightly longer. Even now, 207 years later, the "Preface"
to the *Lyrical Ballads* can be read as a fart of the spirit. Walking
down to a lake both is and recognizes gravity.

And if the lake be frozen over and the walker no longer young and daring,
gravity takes on an added slice of life's bread, leavened with
mortality

Rising only to die of a yeasty hubris. The sink behind the caretaker's
cottage shivers and slides to one side arhythmically just as the
yodel's last note descends

From the *lay* to the *who* of an owl dundiddle-aying above Blue Tarn
(where, only last year, a melancholy man in a graveyard had
discovered an ancient representation of justice

Half-buried and overgrown with moss. It was not blindfolded, it was
armless, like Venus de Milo, and whether it was local or hopeful
was a virtual telescope. Melancholy

Or not, the man could not restrain his impulse to tell his friends about it.
He called Fred Khaled, Joaquin Jones, Joan Robertson-Agoian,
Roger Ahn Phan until sound and sense and the failure of his
cellphone battery

Cut him off). Canoers seek truth on Blue Tarn. Not far away lies a high-
country marsh, dense with mosquitoes, and to the West rise the
daunting Eagle Faces.. Coleridge in his lime-tree bower

Might not have known which way to turn. But he'd have found a
"branchless ash, unscreened and damp" on which to cross perhaps
with the aid of imagination, rain, and memory (criss-crossing
wanderers, all three), and we'd have received various strains,

Singing and stringing yet stressful as unleavened dromedary trots, drifting
from a sodden log so ample in itself, but the blister on my heel
isn't as imaginary as a war-embrace of wrestling life and death.

Is essence dance? Is music the imperative? Can question command the
answers it anticipates and then penalize the answerer, sentencing
him/her to sit on top of a flagpole

Exposed to wind? Patriotism stands blocking our view while the poet's
task is partly to pepper it with strange banners, partly to argue for
many different photographs, as it were, "in a half savage country,
out of date."

Documenting differences within a speck of time keeps that speck in the
light AND leaves its identity in the dark, at least for as long as the

poet creates the document

Tracing the travels of the speck, pen cocked or skittering, swirls of
　　　　palette knife or brush, since some poets like to paint, and dance
　　　　determines speech. Differences are just as dear as they are near to
　　　　disappearance, and the voyeuristic

Traveler does not forget her microscope. Ah! the closeup's discovery of
　　　　a bug in a bud only ups the suspense. Such a bug may exude a
　　　　calmative, which would explain the uneventfulness of the whole

Mountainous area through which a creek rages, happily for the leaves.
　　　　Sleepily, like some ancient oilfather watching a fern frond unwind,
　　　　the scribe sketches nerve bifurcations. But in what context

Is this picture a picture, and on what map is it a name for a mountainous
　　　　terrain? "The" becomes accusatory

When a prosecutor presents evidence of any precision or a doctor holds up
　　　　a baby. But in Louis Zukofsky's "Poem Beginning 'The,'" "The" is
　　　　not a magazine at all.

Can you picture God reading *Newsweek*? There's something happening
　　　　around the edges but I refuse to term it "elsewhere" and then
　　　　suddenly the mounting difficulty

Of understanding what a moment's progress might be makes even the
　　　　ubiquitous squirrels stutterstep and the rhythm of the rain

Forces our attention to the elliptical zigzags that draw some of us into and
　　　　leave others of us out of the big picture. Of course it's impossible
　　　　to picture a victory without showing defeat but, just in time, the
　　　　pen runs out of ink

And the neutral nub slowly forces a zone of seeming blankness. The new
　　　　flag is raised, with a lake on it, blue, with ducks, and tiny white
　　　　figures on the far shore.

They appear to be human—a family, perhaps—, or is it only the innate
　　　　anthropocentrism of our species that makes us see this as a human
　　　　group

Rather than a tumble of rocks or a schematic representation of Boyle's
　　　　Law. Approaching a river, a bicyclist must often juggle the
　　　　imminence of fluid,

In all its ramifications, with images of flight, a whiff of cow dung, and the
　　　　music of a marching band,

Its members dressed in Illinois colors and brandishing papier-mâché
　　　　pitchforks. Pompoms shake, batons are thrown so high they
　　　　disappear, the tuba players

Measure their basso profundo yodels as if mourning were high-pitched
and the dying were not going to disappear. Then the bicyclist
notices the notices

Posted on the lampposts and (as she speeds up, then slows again) the trees.
They're printed on peanut brittle, but that's hard to believe. Music
swells again,

But now she sees it comes from the zither set slightly off-center in the lap
of a woman, heavily skirted, who passes her fingertips over birds.
They fly even while perched

Overhead on thickened clumps of nitrogen. Telephone calls aside, both
spirits and people feel coerced to cover their mouths while
laughing, as if being a "good person"

Or a "good spook" couldn't include a few truth-defying guffaws in a world
of slack-jawed mercenaries and tight-lipped spies. Under the lake
sits a submarine

Of sorts. It's small, almost cozy, and clearly homemade. Beside the lake sit
seven salad-eating sisters, but is "vegan" a way of life or a code?
Loons tilt back and crack

The wildest sound now heard in the fog hovering over suburban lakes.
Zukofsky moves to the nominative, "River that must turn full," he
says, followed by an adverbial "after I stop dying," which becomes
song, raising "grief to music"

As the wind in winter might lift a branch, only to let it slip. Such things
happen, but interpret them as simplicity, please, they aren't
symbolic. Reality stretches or breaks, depending on scale, and it's
full of gaps that coincidences

Pretend to fill. The submarine, meanwhile, has bottled messages to send
and it bursts into the Gulf Stream at dawn. The girls along the
railing

Giggle as the sailors finger their machines and one by one the bottles are
tossed into a cinema of shapes. No two messages are the same.

The word "green" dissolves, one says, but who will

Agree?

Crisscross

CRISSCROSS

1/23: Friend Jim's birthday. Give him
"6." He sits awhile, then off he goes.

in the beginning
the relational was merely a
chickadee's tonic fifth from *somewhere* out on
a twig caused by some consonantal friction
in the soup preceding air

1/28: Dreamed I was a classicist. Cold
sky. To be one would be to plunge
into the misty sea. First discussion
with Heike about the Kaspar Hauser
project, after which I ordered
Feuerbach's *Lost Prince*.

the traveler tosses
in the soup preceding air
which she takes as proof of everything
but clarity is not served by classifying
everything as full of everything

2/5: Up "betimes" 5:30. Stomachache.
Thought how I long to see the stars
in daytime as I stumbled through this
glorious, horrible house.

she realizes seeing
everything as full of everything
is close to seeing seeing as full
of realization, or husband full of husband
—as false as it's obvious

2/17: The garden is sodden but the
soil is strong. I note this from the
window. February is no poor halfway
stage. Sometimes I think I can will
seriousness (meaning), and for myself,
at least, and for awhile, I succeed.

something which is
as false as it's obvious
like a broken chair blocks the way
unless it's the mockingbird's raucous
          jackhammer imitation
through which singing sings on

2/24: Almost missed the sunrise.
Whew! What would I have to have
perpetrated to make up for it? Hope
for a big laugh today. I need it.

rhythms run off
through which singing sings on
top of the jerked gravelly base—I'm
speaking of the glacier, the only local
linear crack in brevity's armor

4/3: M is born; a new life—life didn't
miss. In the same part of town, too,
it remains available to fire-eaters and
to quartets of acrobatic kids ("human
pyramids").

light on the
linear crack in brevity's armor
bends in the dark backward of emotion
—everything that is has continuous duration
          though
the time between limits varies

4/11: Phantom pain seems to be diminishing. Just one lively suicide watch though and it's down to newspapers for a day …

4/17: Hairless but swollen limbs—I'm flailing in a dream. I feel a strong and enduring ambivalence thanks to which I'm both able and unable to answer questions put to me. The inquisitor asks: "Do you believe in dreams?"

4/24: I want to see the night but what I wind up seeing is the light. Oh well, prepare for work.

5/3: I've been keeping six caterpillars in a jar; tonight they have disappeared into metallic pods. One speaks of being "in a state of terror"; is it within one (psyche) or is it the world?

5/13: Traveling. Have reached with my consort Pokagon State Park. Is it named after the Potawatomi band or the eponymous chief who held two mating passenger pigeons in his hands?

5/15: Went to the dermatologist and discussed "fighting dragons," the image on the cover of his new book. Also dreamed that I had a dog, it bit me, then a cat carrying a parrot in its jaws came into the yard. Tomorrow I'll release the butterflies.

then I think
the time between limits varies
for a reason and the reason is
simply this that variation always always wins
by the same token nobody

is all variation
by the same token nobody
crossing a roadside ditch some summer day
remembering her life as Pythagoras as ryegrass
grows wildly beside a road

although some things
grow wildly beside a road
grass only partially tamed by Mr. Pythagoras
words if road's meaning may meander and
in fact become a fantasy

and ryegrass itself
in fact becomes a fantasy
I dream and am that very weed
meandering as a person hopping a ditch
in fear—the world's fearful

but also floats
in fear—the world's fearful
in and out, which merely demonstrates how
we dwell midspectrum, so that one would
think balance might come naturally

to those who
think balance might come naturally
to a tightrope walker crossing a crater
waving a handful of money, giddily weeping
—she has dropped everything else

5/25: Whew! Birdwatching can really take it out of you! At any rate, it kept me hopping today. Peanut butter sandwiches and a letter from Aunt Grace.

6/2: To write poetry in English is not the same as having an "English only policy." Instead of worrying, I've been thinking about the novel that Sophie and I are writing; our heroine is capable of being in two places at once.

6/6: Tom and Gloria are stopping in for coffee and toast today. I must wash the dishes. *And* take Anselm out for Mexican. *And* re-cue all the yodeling tapes. As well as "snake" the upstairs toilet. Oy!

6/9: A cold summer wind is playing the neighbors' wind chime and blowing papers off my desk. Now on the floor are the contact sheets from the rolls of film I shot of multiple horizons: lively sea meeting wall of fog meeting pale sky meeting bank of high dark clouds. Checked my chemicals—I can print tomorrow.

6/15: Have been typing my part of an illot-mollo suite done yesterday at 10,000 feet, at Jane's. And suddenly the bird-clock gives off its 7 a.m. "mourning dove" call, which sounds like an archaic icebreaker, lost, sounding its foghorn, feeling its way toward the Northwest Passage.

and I think
"she has dropped everything else—
now she may drop balance and then
what?" but my fears are groundless, as
is my sense of placement

what worries me
is my sense of placement—
things constantly desert the contexts in which
they make sense and instead show up
somewhere else as something else

such as this
somewhere else as something else
leaves, paradoxically, only the blur of motion
as a gauge of identity operating on
itemized correlation with the known

sleeping in paradoxically
itemized correlation with the known
I dream and think things must refer
—to change: we must outrun the forces
of destruction—as Scalapino says

but the forces
of destruction—as Scalapino says
force us to "wreck our minds" continuously
and rely on some slant regenerate vitality
better we than they, she

6/27: I'm on New England time and
wide awake though dawn in California
is some time off. I brought back two
rocks (each about the size of an Idaho
potato) that I picked up off the beach
on Cape Cod, spotted as I was walking
with two friends, one of whom was
describing the difference between an
estuary and a neutral embayment.

he, it, I—
better we than they, she
or you—yes, better we than you!
it's as "we" that we share existence
with everything—unless it's dreamt

7/2: 6. Sunny, clear early summer
morn poised between warm and cool
so perfectly that when I discover
there's a power outage (Susie-next-
door's all-year Christmas porch
lights are out too) I feel blindsided
by imbalance, like finding a cinder
in an innocent bowl of ice cream.

unless it's one
with everything—unless it's dreamt
in those overlapping ontological scales that
     serve
us up original color schemes (like Matisse's)
wherein difference escalates into identity

7/11: Windows open to another
almost cold evening. Have been
thinking about Schopenhauer's
remark that only a person who gives
love will receive it, but I know several
unloving people who are much loved.
Schopenhauer, apparently, loved no
one.

sun becoming sea
wherein difference escalates into identity
calmly—things are indeed paradoxical and
     paradoxically
composed they experience drama without
     anything's seeming
to occur (like Cézanne's apple)

7/16: Opened up my old file cabinet,
began throwing most of the old
papers into recycle. Got to render
my history lighter, but what if "they"
suddenly reach back through my
head, wanting social security and tax
documents from the 1980s? Reading
Benjamin aloud (but sotto voce).

sports car parked
to occur (like Cézanne's apple)
magnetizing eyes—somehow I think of a
song and dance routine about the protobacteria
meanwhile, summer squirrels chase tails

7/21: Worked on films all day. I like the concept of "shooting the connection," although the phrase, out of context (and certainly my "films" don't provide a cinematic context), sounds as if it refers to gunning down a drug dealer. At the normal 24 frames per second, my films would each last for 6.66666666 (… ∞) seconds; infinitely long.

7/27: Another day of plaster, white paint and above all dust. Movement of objects. Scraping of objects. Glue. Also bank signing and proofreading of tunnel poetry.

8/1: Each frame of the day appears suddenly. The rapidity and brevity with which each is perceived is relative, and some aren't seen at all. Of the 1036800 frames to this 12-hour day, I saw most vividly the doctor's pale feet in sandals and the emerald green dress of the postal clerk at the bulk mailing center. She greeted me as if she knew me.

8/6: Yesterday I drove through the great mountains, tired/wired in my little gray Honda. They loomed and seemed to heave slowly about me, like shoulders shrugging (dancing?) as I descended into the pool of lights. Argued about the price of a hamburger in a Leadville joint called "Wild Bill's."

indoors until evening
meanwhile, summer squirrels chase tails
if they were butterflies they'd browse or
if they were bagging groceries at Safeway
they would see people "squirrel"

their "nuts"—also
they would see people "squirrel"
about in the mock trees our economy
has jerrybuilt, branches like dwindling
    sugar forks
disguised by evanescent green sheets

greed can't be
disguised by evanescent green sheets
though fear of it masks itself and
we imitate ourselves imitating helicopters
    and hover
helplessly—but we make noise

like chickadee life
helplessly—but we make noise
in the, in the tree, in the
tree that, in the tree that quickly
clothes itself with a series

8/12: On a page I've dampened with a wet rag I drew a set of intersecting lines using "slate blue" and "saddle brown"—the resulting image is meant to signify "intersecting undertakings" but I am calling it "Slate Blue: A Western Adventure." I can't draw horses that don't look like manatees.

that repeats and
clothes itself with a series
in whose variations we (not all but
some of us) expect the solace of
continuous expectation—shock, knowledge,
    memory

8/24: The situation is coming to a head: up at dawn, but my delicate tilt into a barely populated world of nascent light is poisoned by the rhythmic whines of the poor old cat.

and violation of
continuous expectation—shock, knowledge,
    memory
in their antimatter avatars—is part of
this humorous whole, too—we find them
tumbling like lovers through each

8/30: Up late last night long after the guests had gone home in the silent light of the lamp above the green table on which the films are spread. Today not so much tired as withdrawn: a quiet day of interior excitement, overcast skies.

coil and column
tumbling like lovers through each
comma of the shifting commentary and
    shadow
of the shaking figure that recognition takes,
humor being what it isn't

9/9: These days I serve as secretary for the incandescent phrasings of tots. But two nights ago the backyard overflowed with bottleneck guitar.

did I say
humor being what it isn't
or is it that … quiver in which
the arrows bend and find their mark
in the smallest possible curl

9/16: When I was in Minnesota last week I walked several times to the Mississippi and sat on a rock, watched the current, called it brown though it was in fact green, and listened to conversing passersby, one woman saying emphatically, "I was honest because I am angry."

huge river turning
in the smallest possible curl
forward—let's draw water as we await
nightfall, says the hunter descending the lock,
or so we imagined, waving

9/21: Walk the McClintock with
friend. Overtaken by Mary with
large black dog and Paul Bowles tales.
Merrill spots two Cooper's hawks
tumbling along distant ridge: the
only migrants.

canes or canoes
or so we imagined; waving
hair's a claim, though, of impending dendrites
in the brain, but branching's not waving
to straw men nothing matters

10/16: Traveling these past several
weeks, thinking about motion. I
don't suppose we could perceive
anything without it (the motion of
the perceiver as well as the perceived).
Saw the leaves turning in New
England, colors moving hour by hour,
beginning to the north and going
south.

sailing over sandbars
to straw men nothing matters
more than anything else and anything else
and anything else matters more than anything
left high and dry, transcendent

10/24: Today (yesterday, now) I asked
one group to write "My Life, starting
tomorrow" and then pass the papers
around to be filled up. Strange how
familiar the chaos resulting from
this orderly shuttle!

such as itself
left high and dry, transcendent
but then you just let them alone
and they become real, carved of wood
you lean back, light up

11/1: The stately hills have their heads
in the hurled rain. Lighthearted
liberation: the appeal of the everyday
is increased. But the emotions should
never serve as a guide to a famous
place.

the stage where
you lean back, light up
this stage of life, the next, "late"
and extreme, all out, we can't give
up the "continual conceptual rebellion"

11/7: Driving through snow recently,
I would have stopped but couldn't
find a light, much less a town, so
kept on my never-joining tracks in
blankness. Election Day.

though crying out
"up the 'continual conceptual rebellion'"
in moments of stress, or moments of
necessary comfort in near-repetition, and
    wondering concomitantly—
is this stress's antithesis or

11/13: I "only have a minute," I say, stopping out of curiosity nonetheless. I don't want to miss anything, don't want anything to miss me. It's a problem. So I "check" the ongoing election news, hear a Florida citizen declare that the election process should be infallible "now that we're in the millennium."

11/19: Woke up yesterday in St. Francis, drove to the Front Range, "playing" old songs. Did laundry, grocery-shopped, watched video of Langston Hughes. Rough-legged hawks are moving through the plains.

11/29: The sun is out among great clouds this morning after heavy rain all night. The light is changing constantly, ghosting the garden like an emissary sent by a dreamer to her dream. I'm going to a party at Tom and Leslie's tonight, taking chocolate mousse, which I have yet to make.

12/2: Days are outpacing my writing hand; yesterday was a curious rubble of love and neglect. Today, I hope, will be like the head of a drake mallard flying off a pond.

12/17: In the produce aisle, near the leeks, the carts of two tall elderly gentlemen gently collide. "What do you think of Bush as President," says one. "Great thing," says the other, take my word for it." "Unh-hunh," says the first, "have a nice Christmas."

synthesis, I ask,
is this stress's antithesis or
a strange tranquillity, an uncontrollable
    refulgence, a
furious oddness that we fear, fearing it
will strand us, draining away

from that that
will strand us, draining away
but coming again and again until "away"
is redefined as part of "here," until
"will the circle be unbroken?"

yes, the song
"will the circle be unbroken?"
comes back on in a hiphop version
or performed by the Mormon Tabernacle
    Choir
—beware! circles can form nooses

and even now
—beware! circles can form nooses
I feel the perfect beauty tighten around
my neck—only universe is big enough
to shake a leg in

cold winter wind
to shake a leg in
came surprising me, I all but tripped
slowly—espousing intransigent, intuitive
    slowness—hurrying to
visit Flaubert, overlooking the surf

12/23: The first drop of sunrise reminds me to awaken my stepdaughter. Clock ludicrously produces titmouse song while hand points to mourning dove.

12/30: Late night at the end of the year brings amazing optimism. It's not that one can choose freedom, it's that one has to. That's all freedom is—the choices required of one.

1/5: My daughter and I listen to biphonic songs from Tuva (she gave me for Christmas), simultaneous drone and melody, "composed of overtones formed by changing the shape of the mouth cavity," various bodypart resonators.

1/10: My daughter and I listen to a message masked by static on the answering machine. It's hard to decipher, she thinks the accent is Russian and the message for me, I think it is French and not for me but for L. L listens next and is able to put it in context because it is from someone he knows: a musician in Moscow.

1/23: I'm in Paradox for two weeks, where the seeming cross-purposes of the river and the valley turn out to be simply, logically, harmlessly that: cross-purposes.

that repeatedly does
visit Flaubert, overlooking the surf
in order to follow the rhythms of
an irregular heart—what would the parrot
think? what would it suggest

if it could
think, what would it suggest
to some young girl one December night
at the beginning of the last century
before the first world war

her virgin metaphor
before the first world war
when clash of arms embraced the globe
and we could feel love history's hands
folding anthropological plate tectonics
    bumping

would have depicted
folding anthropological plate tectonics
    bumping
against the crannies that love invades as
love and abandons as wanderlust—the
    metaphor
of asymmetries, inequities, off-balance
    towers

overwhelms the reality
of asymmetries, inequities, off-balance
    towers
(while seeming to duplicate it) with its
gravity dances: alabaster fault, salt, paste,
    water
all collapsing the various textures

153

1/31: I have reason to believe that I'm going to be offered a "real" job. I don't want to say anything about it. Rae, Travis, mara, Summi, Jeff, and I had a drink together last night in the back room at Dalvah and talked over the music about social activism, protest— louder and louder.

2/14: Another heavy snow. I call Aurora to postpone my appearance, and turn to devote the morning to papers and hearts and photographs.

2/22: Woke at dawn having dreamed two lines—as Nestor to his beloved Lethe, / Lethe, Lethe, all the rest I forget.

2/27: And again snow, a disappointed Aurora. I begin to fear too many delayed dawns might cause a buckled axis …

3/7: The horizon has cleared. The distinction between "recognizable to friends" and "unrecognizable to myself" has a literary history. See Shakespeare, see Stein. See me.

3/13: Aurora. Sense that the Philosophes are streaming above my head, heading out over the Great Plains. Raw carrots. Need a carwash. Think of Juan Lugo: "Open your mind to the / Universe and / Run back home and get your lunch."

in the mines
all collapsing the various textures
of lives long ago lingering—no, penetrating
still—the child yelled Dark! Dark! Dark!
and the trembling guard laughed

to see such
and the trembling guard laughed
sporting a black eye the size of
Berlin, it seemed, though really it couldn't've
been bigger than simple vision

of dark that's
been bigger than simple vision
can encompass, bigger than complex vision can
fill with the chimeras that elude my
camera with its gaping aperture

and mechanical desperation
camera with its gaping aperture
into which light crawls like a fat
thief but finds itself unable to steal
so leaves a little something

ahead, thief hurries
so leaves a little something
behind—I'm curious, want to know what,
want to experience that, have it, get
over history, meet Diderot, scream

encyclopedic echoes under,
over history, meet Diderot, scream
chiaroscuro screams at him, pour corridors of
true-or-false in all directions, remember the
    main
thing is to transcend reification

3/25: The highpoint of the day, the point at which the day (this one) and I (this one) most vividly (to me) intersected, was on the ground late this afternoon: wet soil, worms, small flowers. Anything we yearn for we call beautiful and think we yearn for it because it's beautiful.

3/31: Light snow. Tomorrow I drive into the San Juans. Must fill the feeders first. Today I get little Josh. We'll probably draw pictures and watch a nature video, and practice reading. Cool, don scarf.

4/9: I'm constantly moving, that's what the living do, remaining convivial and feeling dubious—it used to be that I sought my match in this or that but now (this minute) I'm thinking that a mismatch is pertinent.

4/15: Battle my way through papers with their varying temperatures and boustrophedon tracks and shiny layers of processed mud out somewhere to see the shorebirds.

4/22: Received a letter from J and looked up *boustrophedon*. Went out. Returned. Remembered vividly having vaguely noticed a stranger only minutes before furtively changing clothes in an alley behind the supermarket. Memory has many tongues but has no authenticity.

while staring, the
thing is to transcend reification
as a meteorologist might, watching the sky
for the everchanging transit of vapors, veils,
sky receding through materializing light

in the half-conceptual
sky receding through materializing light
—the scientist returns from a long cup
of coffee to find his experiment-world
     spinning
out of control, and a

patina of chalk
out of control, and a
spreading pool of rainbowing oil, sunlit,
     opaque
so that the painterly and inventive
     astronomers
can screen their strange findings

on the mirror
can screen their strange findings
lamination after lamination building up
     a haze
of replicas and their tendency to plunge
clear through semantics and into

the unknown penetrating
clear through semantics and into
history, an opening in belief through which
experience squeezes just as images squeeze
     through
the retina, past motes, scum

4/28: Rehearsed the dwindling group
of facts I maintain to keep up the
illusion of knowledge. The jug-band
luminary's pseudonym seems secure,
but Locke's key premise is out the
door (slam!).

5/1: Dreamed again of papers. These
were spread out on the ground and
were from an encyclopedia, the entry
on "sunset." A caption, "The press of
sunset," was inserted under a drawing
of a man on a ladder repairing a roof.
Seeing it I felt strong emotions and
some perceptions—they are the sole
basis on which I can speak of this.

5/9: Troubled lately by a combination
of coughing and nosebleeds. The
coughing catalyzes the nosebleeds,
which in turn cause me to swallow
phlegm (afraid to blow it) as well as
blood; hence there's a lot to cough up.
One of those spirals.

5/22: Are you okay, Jack? I've been
working on your book. You say
credibility has to be reestablished at
every point. I say products of
the imagination should be granted
more credibility. What a nice example
of conversation—whose twining
spirals I hope will prevail over your
coughing and bleeding.

5/27: I'm fine now, thanks, Lyn, and
you? Went birding, you know, in
south Texas, and today's the big
running race right by our door. How
do you suppose this poem should be
read? Across? By columns? "Around"?

to the brain
the retina, past motes, scum
and retsina's leveling hue, loses its grip,
images flare and tumble onto preliminary
　　Cartesian
screens, and before you know

it there are
screens, and before you know
what they shield, what they show, the
light that's tale-telling flickers, slowing
　　thrown shadows
and the lives they carry

out of sight
and the lives they carry
(provisionally flat) make them come "alive"
　　there
representing time and space as they are
spooneristically shuffled in the glare

like hens who've
spooneristically shuffled in the glare
of a signing sun, a climbing rock
which was long ago a rhyming clock
they cluck, broodily laying eggs

with no recognition
they cluck, broodily laying eggs
in the hands of ladies, or in
the lands of Hades—in either case
the world's a bit warmer

6/3: I wouldn't want to dictate a
"should" to the reading of this poem.
I know for certain that you wouldn't
want to do so either. But I myself read
it as a poem of parallels, which never
quite meet (after all, you and I haven't
met in several years), and yet consist of
converations—meetings.

and smaller! *therefore*
the world's a bit warmer
—because it's compressed, and the
    pressure heats
things, hurries them, speeds time,
    becomes "virtual"
replicating dreams of transcendent sublimity

6/10: Ah, parallels!! On the surface
they might seem like duplicated
effort, but this morning silence
and radiation combine to create a
wonderful soundwave that includes
underground shape.

zero, one, two
replicating dreams of transcendent sublimity
interspersing dactylic runs with words of one
lovely syllable—hut, two, three, four; who
is marching outside the door

6/14: We all bandy the word "stress"
about, it's a hasty shorthand term for
distress. Bolts get worn down,
nuggets worn away. Romantic
introspection dissolves reality in a
mood. To survive—even to exist—
the mood, however, requires absence
of inhibition (solitude).

the future's army
is marching outside the door
—cut to slow motion horserace, calm eye
of a running horse, lid falls, lifts—
denying victory—then everything
    disappears

6/27: Just back from *another* trip, to
Arizona for the literature/environment
conference. I loved it! I was so excited
I spit. Glad I could do that (the
conference) one time in my life.
Now what?

into a gun
denying victory—then everything
    disappears
bang! a new world starts and immediately
complicates itself—finding a meditative
        nook, I
guess is like juggling presence

7/2: Rahel Varnhagen, on reading
Goethe's prelude to *Faust*, commited
the future of her history to it. "They
would carry her with them into the
future. And so it is: again and again
that rhythm will carry us away, carry
us along to the place where those who
come after us, no matter what they
are like, will learn what we know."
(Hannah Arendt, *Rahel Varnhagen*).

and memory I
guess is like juggling presence
—histories "of private things given
        objectivity by
being communicated, public things
    counting only insofar
as they have private significance"

7/15: Naropa summer's over again. I feel a bit like Joseph K might have felt had he been tried before the jury of creatures in *Alice in Wonderland* and then squeezed through Keats's "Ode on a Grecian Urn."

7/22: Even as a child I was driven by a sense that "my days were numbered" or that "time will run out." The concomitant sense, not of regret but of urgency, is based on a set of assumptions (that life is real, that reality is worthwhile) and a question (does one best serve life immediately [e.g., as a doctor] or less evidently and mostly later [e.g., as a writer]).

7/29: Why doesn't anybody pay attention to the "partly" idea? It's so simple: everything is complex "beyond words." The sumac leaflets seem to slice that cloud. I look and look and nothing moves, then look down and when I look up the cloud is gone.

8/3: Assigned to a conference panel whose title is "Poetry & Life," I try to write out some appropriate remarks. I say, "I am neither a neoPlatonist who views this as a shadow world nor a Buddhist who views it as an illusion." I observe, "We have words for reality before we experience it."

8/11: I think of the chickadee, suddenly, become so common now and yet never generalized, as an emblem, as a sort of sneeze, in the smooth August anxiety. Also so reminiscent.

of certain measurability
(as they have private significance
always but typically that significance
    flashes below
the conscious threshhold and does no more
than create the "heaving protoplasm

of moodiness" rather
than create the "heaving protoplasm
of fine sand" sent skidding over hammered
plywood into legible or imaginable shapes) but
of uncertain identity—maybe birds?

are birds questions?
of uncertain identity—maybe birds?
they say they're either the souls of
the recently living or messages from death
depending on rise or fall

accompanying vulnerable travelers
depending on rise or fall
of highways going West under their
    companionship
which travelers accept as promising a long
and lucky life after all

else has evaporated
and lucky life after all
pretty well covers it—but what does
luck mean? now that we "have" it
it seems like a door

158

8/25: Hans Christian Andersen is taken very seriously by poets in Denmark—I asked and was told so. His language is vivid. "Now listen!" he would say, "Listen just for the pleasure of it." His swan like your chickadee is not an emblem but an experience, a memory.

an incredible thing
it seems like a door
swinging on its hinge; happiness enters, grief
enters too, and just then the cat
bolts—men can't fly either

8/31: An incredible thing. It seems like a door. It's a book! Happiness enters. I can fly. I am so lucky, like the Steadfast Tin Soldier, to be caught in a book!

—consider nuts and
bolts—men can't fly either
heavenward or otherwise unless they screw on
wings and—what the hell—go through
a series of explicit steps

9/18: Dan Rather says there are sleepers in our midst. Also bees to be "smoked out" and rabbits to be "hunted down" and "killed in their dens." How strange that beekeepers and foxhunters should be providing the warmongers' metaphors.

poetry still provides
a series of explicit steps
into alien territory where sweet meats are
laid out on blue platters but in
history hunger is the consequence

10/3: In Gunnison Elementary School office planning four hours with 5th graders: haiku, "things to do," illôt-mollo, and "on poetry." Full moon. Diet Coke.

of a blueplate
history hunger is the consequence
of heartless repetition but poetry's a strange
attractor—what a difference a little difference
can spin back and forth

11/12: Geography inch by inch. Rain then and I told some lies. Went to the Cezanne Club. There's no defense for the incomprehensible—that's what can't be understood. This took a lot of time.

we go, we
can spin back and forth
like boats past machines in a pan
shot by the camera man at hand
who's here because it's beautiful

11/20: I help lug huge bundles of arts papers to distribution center. Then lie on couch and listen to first play of new tape olio—it seems to weave the various weathers.

to say whichever
who's here because it's beautiful
like palms "too palm tree, too lanai"
and I see you open your hand
out flies a berry cake

11/30: The Stein seminar has only
one more week to run. I've just
reread "Doctor Faustus Lights the
Lights." Stein liked Satie. I'm
listening to Scriabin. The lamp
behind me is dim. Outside it's cold,
windy, the moon is full.

12/8: Yesterday I wrote a Pearl Harbor
haiku. Today took a Walden/Sawhill
"pond" walk. Read all the Writing
Outreach essays, and I wonder what
happens to kindness in chaos.

12/18: Shame, elation, anxiety, pride:
one discovers the dividedness that
comprises oneself, the dividedness
without which one would never be
capable of experiencing oneself nor
individual death. Cavemen love.
Today I wrote.

12/25: Today, after distraction and
labor, an equipoise of what to do and
nothing else. Beginning with a large
potato breakfast, then exploding in a
cloud of wrapping paper and chin-
music.

1/7: Old fears in my thought, new
life to mind, unmindful of me. The
suffusing emotions go into the blue,
but now Diego is here. Winter harbors
the sources and properties of spring.

1/21: Back from the Big Apple and its
ruddy round emanations from gray
orthogonal. Such a warm paradox!
Poetry business. Snow geese, red-
breasted mergansers. Lost in Brooklyn.
White-throated sparrows.

with a wave
out flies a berry cake
from a floating lake—with such expertise
as from swamping laughter and
        flying mistakes
beloved faces have been made

conscious of what
beloved faces have been made
of, and it turns out to be
a substance I can't quite put my
finger on, although sometimes I

type, book open,
finger on, although sometimes I
am reluctant to say so, a phrase
so persuasive I take it for mine
written earlier, on December 17

on the radio,
written earlier, on December 17
it flew, mock-extempore, into a
        thousand ears
as if the only stability were an
explosion, and the only explosion

were this, an
explosion, and the only explosion
experienced only from the first only once;
aphorisms alone apply and they seldom do—
such wonders are paradoxically abundant

as Chinese boxes
(such wonders are paradoxically abundant)
and with that I go out to
feed the inner self, which in turn
discharges into the outer layers

2/4: Two young uneasy wishful women
met, one by one. A paleographer, the
first, protested that an A from one
pen might be a D from another. I am
not Richard Brautigan, the second
explained, and I am not a connoisseur
of cherry trees.

all this that
discharges into the outer layers
—dust, a temporal pathos, the little girls—
does so with its own sudden individuality:
chaos—existing must be illogical

2/14: Pre-dawn of Valentine's Day.
Would it were ever thus. Yesterday 5
sessions at a Denver middle school
with African-Americans and their
superior poetic impulse.

thus we have
chaos—existing must be illogical
but still, windows of perfect repetition occur
and then are swallowed up again as
if crazy spiraling were all

2/24: The they of "their" is the we of
us under the press of a "superior poetic
impulse." Not for a single moment is
there silence. Electricity hums, blood
drones, we trip over impediments and
share the laugh as I skin my knee "like
a girl" skating by.

that there is
if crazy spiraling were all
there is no repetition in the air
none heard though we hear the word
1000 times it's always new

3/5: What I'd thought was silence
turns out to be a "tiny" world spinning
behind my cough medicine, and I
suddenly realize I have a 9 a.m. job at
a "junior academy," followed by blue
yodel practice.

new new new
1000 times it's always new
even to the point of taking on
an infant dream's shiny blue tubular uniform
since the universe is curved

3/16: The concert was about to begin.
G and I filled the water whistles and
passed them out. The nightingales and
cuckoos were ready. The Polish violist
conducted the toy symphony. M sat—
I gazed with Proustian longing. There
is no flattery in it.

it's loopy too
since the universe is curved
and hilarity in the infant's dream carries
good spirits to excess—she throws
     buckets
of water into the air

3/22: Wonder how long I'll live. Oh
well, I hear a blue jay calling "Here!"
and remember last night freewriting
on the subject of "Carnival" with the
boys at AIM-house.

4/6: It's she who went, and her hand,
17 days ago, that I hopelessly watch for
now. With the others who watch, too,
we speak of commas. How, then, free,
might writing, there, nowhere, be?

4/20: A cold morning for a birdwalk.
Hitler's birthday. I'd better eat that
banana before it's too late. This would
make a very interesting soup, I think.

4/27: The plot is beginning to unfold
and we see something fascinating:
someone is born and lives day by day,
doing this and that, into old age—and
that's the point. The whole thing's a
mystery. Who did it?

5/16: I came early to Kent this
morning to check the Highline Canal
for warblers but no luck. My third
and last visit. Kelly the teacher wrote
of both poetry and photography as
"distillation of big life into sheets."

5/23: A band of morning sunlight
touches the bookshelf to my left.
What I see there is not "a body of
work" but action. The books are on
the shelf only to make way for more
action. Clutter would get in the way.
Go, little books!

and also antitheses
of water into the air
until the air has become quite solid
or, more accurately, has gone somewhere
        else
and left a weighty toy

which, broken, fell
and left a weighty toy
—we call it human, mortal, we're
        careless
with it—I had one but now
it's gone, and its hand

belies the fact
it's gone, and its hand
has left any number of motions divisible
by five, as well as several starfish
I'm saving with their sand

from different rocks
I'm saving with their sand
to set among the dangling wisteria beans
which are actually shadows in a dish
I'd like to hand her

luscious pearls and
I'd like to hand her
over to the authorities for swallowing
        valuable
material and metamorphosing it into
        curves of
dots and dots of curves

along coasts continuing
dots and dots of curves
around shapes that then escape as death
escapes life and life death, six, seven
—numbers preserve intensities: hours,
        pearls

5/29: Sierra's here! Heralded by a
golden-winged warbler in the
"jungle" below the University. But
Stephen Jay Gould has died at sixty.
Yes, "Go, little books!"

6/3: A bird appears with a rapidity
that awakens the camera. Its future
is its past. Death makes no appearance
and deprives us of those who used
to appear. But the sun is bright, the
hollyhocks are huge. "Flower, you
flowers, and flourish!"

6/12: Into an open Buddhist cell
pour mitochondria from all over, for
example a wonderful dark Caribbéan
voice named McMorris. In the
morning, I lead a young group through
pond country; we surprise an egret.

6/20: Babies are insistent, free of
idealism. But the six (!) lasted through
Dvorak's "Songs My Mother Taught
Me." I said, "Life never got old for
her" and "We start—anew—in the
world—she taught us."

6/29: And a wonderful poet just died,
having said he'd "like to be laid on a
bed of frozen strawberries." Two early-
morning magpies make an incredible
din as I write this.

7/8: He said, "What if everybody did
that?" He knew that they do: "LIMIT
defined by change of state." It doesn't
take all that much to encourage
oneself. It took less than a mile from
any given parking lot, less than a few
minutes out. L smiled.

and doublings, flesh
—numbers preserve intensities: hours,
        pearls,
meanwhile, coincidence preserves the
        mechanics of breath
even though I'll die when I learn
repetition stands on its head

blown, down, grown—
repetition stands on its head
in the flow of sound; the clowns
go round, the birds bow; who knows
how—welcome, clowns, to town

even Tonto says
how—welcome, clowns, to town
trumpet toots tandaradei, then mock nativity
        turns
inside out and all the dead are
born again, to try out

anticipation without being
born again, to try out
expectation as itself an end, escaping end—
but I can't do that—not being
a clown—not wearing paint

does not unmake
a clown—not wearing paint
simply means one has drunk the paint
and will pour it out when skin
breaks, to cheers and rosy

smiles—shaken decoration
breaks, to cheers and rosy
death, which we did not consider, strings
across blast, long hours—we submit
        ourselves
someplace else, looking at it

7/18: Last night at the West End Tavern, progressive jazz and thrice-divergent words, quick watercolor paintings, a woman sitting for her portrait. A late night. Energy chiefly red, yellow, black and gray.

7/29: I composed a couplet for a bed-and-breakfast guestbook in my sleep. I rhymed "heavy with fog" with "slept like a dog" and woke laughing. Past and future both tear at the present. It's not enough to deny that.

8/14: About to go to Mexico for ten days I come down with diarrhea. Is it the body cleverly one-upping *turista* or simply a prophetic melting away? Time will tell.

8/19: Resemblance can't be the measure of all things. I heard a puzzling man say that it's from language that humans learn the concept of deceit. For his example, he said that he had arrived on Friday and would leave on Friday a day later.

8/28: In the homecoming jet I ate my screaming-with-sugar snack and read Peter Coates, in his book *Nature* (which wraps around me like a swim in the Caribbean), quoting Plato's characterization of the world of matter as a tomb.

9/5: On my desk at dusk on a scrap of paper an imagined figure, the fatalistic Lola, has written, "Before I existed I was already at work on myself—I was born prepared."

while the specificity's
someplace else, looking at it
in such a way as to highlight
the incongruity by nearly fitting "it" to
itself—and then where do

hours, time asks
itself—and then where do
these hours come to rest like cups
in an earthquake, flung, spun, and cracked
against the foreground's five-word line

over a hillock
against the foreground's five-word line
again—these painfully individuated
      hours enduring double-duty
space?—my memory grinds against
      my desire
like minutely varying tectonic plates

something like this—
like minutely varying tectonic plates—
we give and take, for the sake
of "something" that shakes, chair or
      needle
—something in any case real

as a dash
—something in any case real
as motion (which resembles being in every
way but one (although there's "something"
      about
it that seems to, I

think, be really
it that seems to, I
guess (no less than "I" when I
think I am) produce effects (which are
all there is of it)))

9/11: September 11th at Elk Creek
Elementary quite nice: only a tiny
fraction of the day's breeze was
tragedy rhetoric. I had a bloody nose
when I arose, played eightball with
my host in the evening.

9/19: The rightwing stole the public
9/11 and now flaunts it but I'll have
no part of it. I called M to wish him
a happy birthday. I left the message
with A. The next day the children
encountered a rattlesnake at the door;
I could hear it rattle from 150 miles
away. A and M netted it and freed it
two miles away.

10/19: Last night I went to the
LaFonds' house; they'd hired me to
lead a dozen guests in some poetry
exercises, followed by pool. Such fun!
And a gram of guilt that I took money
for sheer enjoyment. But if there must
be money, it must be for that. The gift
of options, given to the optional. Work
not enjoyed might be paid for in bags
of wild rice.

10/26: Philip Whalen told Joanne
Kyger that poetry is to be practiced,
every day, like play. And just as the
little girl playing in the shade with
plastic animals would never think
to ask if the play was "good" or even
"the best she could do," so the poet
shouldn't ask such questions of her
poems.

three arcs and
all there is of it
blows away the crisscross denoting deep
        versus
ready to embrace to emphasize I guess
the girl with the golden

hoop: out jumps
the girl with the golden
pony named Sam, short for Something
        Always
Matters and she takes off horizontally
        wildly
in concert with Sam's adverbs

inevitably growing louder
in concert with Sam's adverbs
such as nattily, grainily, explicitly, and well
and she thinks, "What would life be
in an adverbial world?" Suddenly

we begin, "each
in an adverbial world?" Suddenly
sure: ordinarily obvious embraces scarcely
        slowly noted
unfold and the fairytale energy intensifies,
        terrifying
greatly the goose—it flies

11/3: 4 a.m. of a Sunday, and yesterday J and I arose early and with sleepover Josh (8) drove to Westminster, from whence Wahid drove us to Manitou Springs, where J was involved in a play, Wonder Tales of the Islamic World. Pizza for lunch, and during the second performance Josh and I wandered along the street, wherefrom I purchased him a pair of *cool* dark glasses.

parts of it
greatly the goose—it flies
the various portions painfully ratcheting
    up a
semblance of togetherness, like a meal,
    and
suddenly I am hungry so

11/14: Indeed as I write this (at 8 p.m. of a Thursday) I *am* hungry and for the first time in a week, and I think it may be symbolic (in a Freudian sense): a mourner has suffered "a loss with respect to an object"; the depressed has suffered "a loss with respect to his or her ego." There's no real antithesis here, but I'm a mourner not a depressive, and the potatoes are baking.

after hearing harps
suddenly I am hungry so
grievously that the harps seem near, the
birds far from the confusion, the storm
clouds neither hard- nor soft-hearted

12/8: Yesterday early I went to King Soopers to pick up some photographs and chocolate milk, and the nearest little ornamental tree embedded in the sidewalk in the parking lot gave forth a high sound. I looked: cedar waxwing singing. Thought of asking Customer Service if they had any cedar waxwings, but the man would've only said, "I'm sorry, sir, we're out of that item."

but simply harped
clouds neither hard- nor soft-hearted
in the sense that the food they
provide is utterly practical and the joy
I feel is purely "animal"

12/12: Walking north through Berkeley this morning, I had to cross an intersection partially blocked by a cement truck. "Worth your life to get anywhere in this world," said a fellow pedestrian. "But as my mother always said, 'you aren't healthy til you're sick.'" Transitions are not always indicative of progress.

the steady rainfall
I feel is purely "animal"
and that is just as the Stoics
would have felt it—coming all together
in connected sentences, conjugating fate

12/20: We haven't seen "our" screech owl perched on an off-kitchen window ledge awhile now. But why should he always do the same thing? I haven't been to the corner coffee shop in a week or more either, but I'll get there again.

as if alive
in connected sentences, conjugating fate
but not to a series of recommendations
so much as to a musical notation
which is not perfectly steady

12/26: We are here and these are our times. What have we done, what are we going to do? My subconscious was an animal and it died but before it did it taught me to incorporate the phrase "it's no big deal but …" into sentences. E.g., it's no big deal but people are standing like statues, benumbed, or, as a last resort, they're screaming.

but it's beautiful
which is not perfectly steady
nor is the instrument—impossible to
    tune it
all knowledge of it being deeply hidden
—but no revelation is self-sufficient

1/1: Up at 5 today, out to Walden/ Sawhill. Heard great horned owl, then went for coffee. Back and walked the refuge, counting 27 species of birds, ecstatic (me) though the ponds were mostly grotesquely "chapped." And I know the aquifer's sucking down fast.

I can't hear
—but no revelation is self-sufficient
thanks—or it would be formed like
a revelation, which is megaphone-shaped
    and red
or so I envision it

1/7: The place was called Antarctica but we knew it was Norway because we'd been there in that very (beautiful) landscape. Reveling in the sense of recognition (or superiority) I dashed out naked into the icy landscape. Groups of children, all in red caps, watched, making sure that I knew I was out of place.

between clowning clouds
(or so I envision it)
the shadow of a single day—or
is it just a waggling stick—hits
the horizon: there's a ship

1/16: Years ago I'd go up to Blackhawk regularly and lead writing workshops for a group of pattern painters called Criss-Cross. The best poetry, I think, was tossed off orally by my young son Chris as we rode in the back of somebody's pickup. I failed to write it down because I didn't feel it was proper to self-consciously ground his flights, and now I don't have it (nor does he), except in transformations.

suddenly diving through
the horizon: there's a ship
we won't see again, unless of course
we become treasure hunters, plumbing
        the repetition
fluidity typically seems to allow

1/21: After three weeks of it, I've given up writing down my dreams. I meant to do so this morning—there was something about my telling my young son Paull to stop crayoning in the books—but forgot and in retrospect, reading over the others, I don't … well, okay, maybe I'll continue, but I don't have any sense of their sense.

practicing, plotting—the
fluidity typically seems to allow
or even to insist that we prepare
for center stage and left and right
getting the elephants to dance

1/31: My daughter called me at noon Monday and we had a lovely hour's her-birthday talk. She's fine but also disheartened by the human world. That evening I heard Molly Ivins on KGNU and wrote for the tape of her remarks. Fiery protests playful and fun; the combination of open and sharp. "Hi, Great White Shark," wrote 6th-grade Anthony Fraticelli, "your fin is like the tooth of a raging vampire…. Your eye is like the cold, dark sky."

as it were
getting the elephants to dance
like the words in a Gertrude Stein
poem—I feel like I'm about a
hundred feet in the air

168

2/9: Dream: none remembered.
Read: some pages from Cooper's
Last of the Mohicans, some pages
from *Capital*; random passages
from Heidegger's *Elucidations of
Hölderlin's Poetry*. Went: with L to see
Morvern Callar. Wondered: how do
we reconcile the fascination with the
object that is central to Zukofsky's
"objectivism" with Marx's critique of
the commodity?

2/21: As I drove toward Denver
yesterday (to appear before a literary
panel judging applicants for a joblet
this summer) about 6-6:30 a.m. the
bare trees were so intensely black
against the dawning sky that their
wildnesses seemed on the point of
bursting clear from their dendro-
forms.

3/2: Last Friday at midnight the INS
ceased to exist, all of its functions
becoming part of Homeland
Security. I was in Kentucky at that
hour talking to Carla Billitteri,
Alan Golding, Barrett Watten,
Ben Friedlander, Barbara Cole.
The occasion was an "academic
conference," the experience at that
hour was of "mind's peace."

3/12: Stan Brakhage died a few days
ago. He fathered, with my sister
Jane, five children, who all flew out
yesterday to Victoria, BC, where his
immediate widow, Marilyn, and their
two sons are. There's too much more
to say.... A chickadee sings its spring
song outside (it's dawn).

fifty up-ended brains—
hundred feet in the air
"and love too affixes attentive eyes"
          upward
to encourage the other—bringing
          restoration
and sensuousness to a thing

can replace it
and sensuousness to a thing
alone can split into pure love and
on the other hand touch, which is
illusory, you know, from electrical

circuits which aren't
illusory, you know, from electrical
points of departure to quick luminous
          velocities
of the type that woke Frankenstein's
          monstrous
man desiring to project mind

onto body of
man desiring to project mind
(well, you know what I mean) so
many times that desire becomes a person
of a kind we can't

3/30: It's late, too late for all that there's to say with respect to the past 15 days which I spent in New England. On the fourth day the U.S. without credible justification went to war. I was sitting on my bed on the third floor above P and L's bedroom at 9:30 pm when P called up, "It's begun, Mom, I'm coming up." We sat side by side on a mattress on the floor of his office in front of the black and white tv. It was all so obviously wrong that there was little to say.

emulate, a person
of a kind we can't
initiate without disaster however clever
        s/he might
be or become by reading newspapers over
people's shoulders on the bus

4/5: As war officially began, I was blizzard-bound in an airport, waiting futilely in line to blurt hopes on a United "red phone"; J is now in Afghanistan distributing basic goods and helping start schools. The world's environment is going to hell (which means a place where harm redoubles harm).

an act which
people's shoulders on the bus
attempt to foil by hunching, though
        some
apparently feel they have to
        accommodate, as
if hospitality were at stake

4/13: The war began again (the war that has existed long enough to exterminate whole species) and with revulsion (the revulsion that has existed long enough to twist our intestines) we protested—and it is these, our protestations, that have to be original, new.

I know that
if hospitality were at stake
there'd be entries in every index to
hosts and guests: "description of,"
        "reciprocity between,"
etc.—to hell with xenophobia!

4/25: Yesterday I drove 70 miles south to Sagewood MS and by the time I got there deep heavy snow covered everything. It kept snowing all day, until I left a little early, not knowing whether the weather varied in time or space. But just ten miles north the countryside lay springbright. The whole way then I listened to lively music from the '20s, cassettes sent me by Bill Koehl.

let's redefine desire,
etc.—"to hell with xenophobia!"
repeated and repeated might make us
        familiar
with the feel of unfamiliarity's cold fear
frying, and then we might

4/28: Evening spring light is coming through the window, it shines on this small square, this image-instant, "the imprint of a once-present and unique moment." I'm listening to John Zorn's *Chimeras*, Ilana Davidson's lyricless vocalese (for which we thought at one point that I should write lyrics and then agreed that I shouldn't).

5/10: Early Saturday May snow postpones the Global Response birdathon. It means I can shovel the blizzard that's on my desk. Finish grading eco-lit thoughts. Cook a turkey-bacon breakfast. Call Kaiser to re-order pills. Bill Young Audiences. Recycle. Read the paper. Take a walk.

5/23: Between my ears memories— echoes and pressures brought on by a virus—extinguish thought—and with it bad news. Deny nothing and all will be denied on your behalf and nothing will come of your denial—of bad news. The sky over the sheep meadows near Roslyn Chapel—I remember that.

5/30: Yesterday I appeared before a grants panel known as SCFD. I'd been dreading it for weeks and weeks because I'd done nothing to prepare— no schools contacted, no funding arranged. But then my ten minutes consisted entirely of the 12 people passing around the children's writing anthologies I'd brought and chuckling gleefully, nay, beatifically.

listen, while potatoes're
frying, and then we might
find it's time we desire, time we
might manage continuously to discontinue
    without losing
time all our own, unmanaged

and wild-eyed, shredding
time all our own, unmanaged
by formal considerations; this means
    managed by
the next layer of form, which perhaps
doesn't have a name yet

vulnerable—impressionable—it
doesn't have a name yet
—it's much like a scrap of glue
left behind by a collagist bound for
Paris with three passion fruits

—imagine being in
Paris with three passion fruits
but without that all-important scrap
    of glue
representing the indeterminate glory
    lying inside everything
thus is the exotic trivialized

6/2: Recovering from a cold in the summer heat attentive to breezes, color, light, I've stuck pretty close to home until the barbecue at H and F's yesterday afternoon. There I fell into conversation with an engineer originally from Iran; he asked me if I knew anything about Language Poetry, said it had all been started in 1950 by a woman whose name he couldn't remember.

commodified, imported, sold—
thus is the exotic trivialized
as the trivial is exoticized, commodified,
   sold
to strangers—they might even be birds
airborne—in a parallel world

6/8: I too went to a barbecue "yesterday" afternoon. No, it was a spaghetti dinner. I took Josh along and we were handed paste-on namecards (it was the beginning of Naropa's Summer Writing Program). Josh wrote "Beef Jerky" on mine, and I wrote "Arthur Rimbaud" on his.

where trivia blooms
airborne—in a parallel world
where it assumes its own atomic nature
and then must labor mightily to be
reduced to a piece of

6/12: If we don't accept time—that is, if we don't accept that everything is fleeting, that everything changes and nothing can be brought back to what and where it was—then we have no sense of history. Catastrophe and pollution are the result.

a puzzle we've
reduced to a piece of
a puzzle we'll deduce from the piece
—then we'll swing in the hammock's web
adrift over puzzled thought's bed

6/20: This morning I attended the SWP class led by Pierre Joris and Nicole Peyrafitte (I've been trying a different one each day—all wonderful). Pierre quoted Mallarmé: "A throw of the dice will never abolish chance." He also gave a teaching tip: have your students read their poems line-by-line backwards.

on the ground
adrift over puzzled thought's bed
under the ground and while down there
we'll hear a scratching sound—is it
something inside wanting out or

6/27: Imagine a film called "The Merry
Month of May"—would it be grim?
The plot might include a murder,
undertaken dutifully, opportunistically,
carelessly, roguishly—but not
timelessly—of a child. A few days ago
I began making this film, drawing
the plot inch by inch, around a pole.
My filmmaking materials include 17
pencils, a very fine pen, and 3 bottles
of black (but different black) ink.

7/1: I started my class. Intro's consisted
of name and "What's funny?" When
things go awry, Sex, Watching my
cat Dali chase light shadows on the
wall, That I forgot something to write
with, Orange marmalade…. 14 people
arranged in a square.

7/7: On 7/5 by the sea the wind was
strong. We thought to try out the
blue diamond-shaped kite and it took
right off, its vivid yellow tail streaming,
to the end of the 500 feet of string.
Then a gust jerked it higher and it
sailed away between seagulls toward
an osprey, we pursued, through grass,
across a little river, along the path to
the top of the cliffs….

7/12: Depths of summer. Not bad.
Chartreuse. I try again to call H., my
Honduran friend in Indiana who is
having a heart by-pass, and again his
line is busy. Yesterday I spontaneously
up and selected 60 or 70 lomo
photographs made in the last half-year.
I call the group "Walking Ground"
and may phone KR at the Library, see
if we can make a show, accompany it
with eco-readings.

are we that
something inside wanting out or
perhaps thumbing our nose at whatever's
    out
"there" between Kenya and the Ivory
    Coast
between Dvorak and Mos Def

between the sheets
between Dvorak and Mos Def
that seem to obscure the absolutely
    passional
near-identity of the "notes" involved,
    that is
to adduce a standing wave

we shout, "wait"
to adduce a standing wave
and show ourselves hospitable and
    surprised—
it being the artists' fate to be
surprised—but of artists alone?

oh, you'd be
surprised—but of artists alone?
is a question wherein that word "alone"
represents the true fuzziness turned
    to stone
in order that the artist

173

7/18: I would like to linger here admiring the long shadows and delightful odors of the afterday. Sitting at my desk early this morning I first heard and then saw a fat mosquito. It landed on the cover of *The Oxford Companion to Ships and The Sea*. I thought of smacking it but decided to give it a break: it wasn't bothering me and I wouldn't bother it. It flew off and a minute later I was driven to scratch the top of my foot, welted in two places.

8/1: For the last 4½ months I've been wearing oxygen tubes. It's like writing sonnets. Last night J. and I watched Attenborough's "The Private Life of Plants" on our VCR. The sense of burgeoning energy in nature was stunning, or, rather, its opposite.

8/5: A great cinematic cut is a beautiful—an awe-inspiring—thing. This morning on my computer Nick Dorsky's *Devotional Cinema* went from Word to Quark. I found myself pulling into a parking space outside Home Depot. Nearby the dry weeds and litter of the median strip were on fire. I ran from the flames with a letter in my hand, but it was a feather.

8/12: A dear one recently visited her very dear 96-year-old dying godmother in the nursing home and sat quietly while the old woman slept. The roommate said, "Oh wake her up—she sleeps *all* the time!" The dear one snapped, "None of your business!" The roommate called her "Miss Smarty-Ass." When the dear one later told, sadly, of the whole visit she laughed at that part.

can shout "surprise"
in order that the artist
can signal to the magician, her assistant,
that it's time—don't ask for what:
it's time that's the surprise

within the repetition
it's time that's the surprise
"the the the" the clouds seem to
say, and blow away, but not before
the pitterpat of rain begins

months pass before
the pitterpat of rain begins
and mud builds—nothing vanishes in this
world breaking the spines of the paperback
book: Tolstoi's *War and Peace*

but look! another
book: Tolstoi's *War and Peace*
too replaces it and we realize that
the thought is too exact for the
reality it seeks to portray

8/18: A lemon squirrel, walnut in
paw and straight out of childhood,
is scolding a darker squirrel in the
redwood tree, or maybe that's not
scolding but naming. If so, I'm not
familiar with the science of it, the
pulling of the squeaking screen door,
the nostalgia, the stand for canes.

pen stroking the
reality it seeks to portray
in a set of square inches sets
chinks in play and catches a fiber
past which it spatters day

8/24: I drove to Ft. Collins to attend
Bill Gore's funeral at the little Unity
Church, 1401 Vine. Paula was gracious
and pretty; 25 family and friends
gathered; the woman minister read
a fine talk, down-to-earth but also
quoting Blake and the Vedas; I read
a poem about our Illinois boyhood
times; his son tearfully, movingly
spoke of how he missed him; another
old pal spoke; everyone said he was
big but gentle, loved cruises; "Amazing
Grace" was played on tape; drove back,
listening to experimental didjeridu
music, stopped for a slice of pizza in
Longmont.

to the end
past which it splatters day
reflected in a strange but utterly familiar
series of Dracula-form atom-doublings
        scattered in play
if play is basic motion

8/29: Three times this week I walked
to work bearing books and noting
trees on one block, construction
workers on another, a crane gently
moving in the breeze. Walking
home again many hours later with
the same and/or different books, I
passed through (or in) a fugue state,
moving from the first block to the
fifth without experiencing 2, 3, or
4—traveling at ease.

it ends but
if play is basic motion
begins in sloshing play near mild fronds
that barely hide the tabby talking cat
—time in the spigot mumbling

9/7: I went to an open house Monday (Mark DuCharme) and had three drinks, then came home in time for dinner with family. I drank two glasses of red wine and became sarcastic to J's daughter S's boyfriend M and my face became terrible (though my memory is one of jollity). He (a muscleman) (quite sober) became enraged and shouted the most extreme physical threats over and over. They left. On Tuesday I called S, learned of my culpability and apologized. M called me and continued his shouted threats, coupled with a strong denigration of my entire life, as he saw it.

passing, even purring
—time in the spigot mumbling
about it all and every mumble is
a world of peace in which microscopic
wars assume enormous slowly-whirling
    forms

9/14: The weather turned hot and I couldn't sleep in the stifling, airless hotel room. The fan roared. I articulated powerful banalities in no uncertain terms expressing love to those I love who were not there or would soon go away. They are no longer here; maybe they never were.

it's unsurprising that
wars assume enormous slowly-whirling
    forms
—their dogged purposes are frustrated by
    barking
dogs howling at their heels and herding
unique microscopic dots with devotion

9/25: Up at 6 and drove to Evergreen (altitude 7800 feet), began residency at "Marshdale" School. 3 classes, typed poems, addressed an assembly, settled in. A 5th-grade girl wrote in response to a Picasso painting (xerox):
"There once was a girl from Perú
Who dreamed she was playing the
    kazoo.
She awoke with a start
To discover that part
Of her was, that her dream had come
    true."
Drove home and attended Reggio's inchoate mass of beautiful pans, "Powaqqatsi."

to their atoms
unique microscopic dots with devotion
in turn into the wholes *into* those
wholes, where the rubbings of scales
    produce
a form of universal barking

10/3: Charles North is coming to
town to give a reading at UC-Berkeley
and in preparation for writing an
introduction to his reading I googled
"Charles North." There are numerous
highschools in America named
St. Charles North and something
about many of them come up on my
computer screen. But Charles North's
poetry is suffused with the presence
(or rather, as he puts it in one poem,
the kennings) of realities that abound
beyond reach of the senses: "Zito's
gold," Wall cookies," "The deflector of
the night's June."

the trees ascend
a form of universal barking
singing in their sunbath, tuned and
          entering
reality into sound's registry as sublime as
sight of trees can be

10/13: Hurly-burly of fall; the (rich)
leaves are still "up"; the Continental
Divide's suddenly white. Columbian
flow. J just turned 57, held a mini-
conference on saving ancient
treasures in war-devastated lands,
and preserving culture everywhere.
Fish. Jokes. I've been writing writing
writing with small children, sexy
youth, and sage 45-year-olds. J begins
raw-food diet tonight.

shaped note style
sight of trees can be
after a non-nature-loving long life an
          utter

"OH!"—including revelation for a
          forgetful lady like
my late mother walking and

10/17: I now live in a state governed
by a terminator. In the parking lot
behind the apartment building a
car door slams and from my room,
windows open, I hear a woman's voice
saying cheerfully, "What" with an
uprising lilt and "ever" with finality.
Was Hamlet driven mad by the
political success of those completely
undeserving of political support?

seeing leaves it's
my late mother walking and
lovely in her feelings as she sees
trees growing causeless in the forest
          blowing
towards her, music, her destination

10/22: In an effort to glorify the quotidian, I ask a New Vista HS class to write "Things to Do…" poems. But my own is about Hamlet, under the guise of "Things to Do in a Story," and ends, "Write how the sun rises in the morning and it's time to start over. Replace crumb into world; pat tenderly. Put microscope away. Have a sandwich…."

10/28: After the false alarm, the fire crew having cleared us to re-enter the building, I said that I wanted to jump over pages of stutter step prose improvisation and darting and diving and sometimes even dancing thought to lines which perfectly replicate the action of a wheelbarrow as it moves into an instant of time.

11/7: Tonight a benefit reading for Akilah Oliver, whose son died last spring, partly because his hospital treatment—for sudden appendicitis—was shamefully delayed. / And now the performance is over and it was superb. Wondering what to say next, I look up at the pictures pinned under my window, particularly at a photo of nude, very earnest, dancing girls from, perhaps, the 1890s.

11/15: They were alive, the bowlers in the photographs on the back wall of the bowling alley in Salinas, very briefly. In the alley next to ours was a sullen woman bowling magnificently. Driving home we heard a radio interview with a famous writer who spoke with piety of having "yielded to the magic" while writing her latest book. Wasn't the woman bowling so perfectly doing the same, and weren't we, driving home?

and hears, blowing
towards her, music, her destination
both caused and causeless, occurrence
    and happenstance,
opening out, circle and rectangle,
    to chaos
dotted with sparks of memory

here's a name
dotted with sparks of memory
blown into wakefulness from a troubled
    dream:
child asleep with a python, a barn—
composite animals: lion-burro, alligator-
    dove, mother-goose

say it again
composite animals: lion-burro, alligator-
    dove, mother-goose
and, not to be stuck with dichotomies,
a magnificent paramecium-porcupine-
    remora-emu-cloudrat-robin-
    (blind)loach happily
    ruling the roost
while trying repeatedly to walk

let's not despair
while trying repeatedly to walk
away—or just the reverse—to stop
a sudden emotion that calls forth tears
from a flight of fancy

178

11/22: At the Ricks Center for Gifted
Children in Denver the 7th and 8th
graders were wonderfully lively and
engaged (almost too lively at times),
in contrast to the opaque "cool" that
envelopes most kids their age. Laura
said that if they were dispersed in
public schools most of them would
"hide." But what a shame to "isolate"
them as a group.

11/25: A northern California winter is
settling in, the moon will be full on
December 8, the heating system in the
house is barely adequate, the university
semester has only one more week of
classes to go. The Graduate Student
Instructors are set to go on strike. I'll
support them and then go east.

12/6: 62 years ago tomorrow I sat with
Mom, Daddy, and Jane in our dining-
room making a Christmas house of
sugar cubes. Suddenly the radio on
the buffet interrupted its flow of light
classical music with an announcement:
Pearl Harbor had been bombed. "Well,
we won't be making any more sugar
houses for awhile," said Mom in her
flat Illinois tones.

12/11: From an attic room on Garden
Street I'm watching a rain fall into
the near dark of a late afternoon in
Cambridge after heavy snow, the light
itself draining away. Across the street
a heavy woman is trying to negotiate
the waist-high banked snow and
curbside slush. I feel suddenly a rush
of clear intuition—anonymous grief,
site unspecified.

down the hill
from a flight of fancy
(they are all around us, like water)
gazing at one thumb, then the other,
far apart but in line

the words appear
far apart but in line
—aardvarks in an alphabet, boxed pasta,
        spoons—
and I'm afraid to cross it, something
awful's on the other side

though they think
awful's on the other side
over there, as they peer through the
surreal stream and then the no-man's-
        land of
opaque whiteness edged with legend

they may find
opaque whiteness edged with legend
—small deeds handwritten in snow
        of souls'
impressions not of servitude but of birds
in shells of goose-like zombies

12/30: For a full week we ten were facing ocean, its plain extreme dichotomy with beach, and finding that simplicity a rollercoaster to the most delightful complications. Shells, mud patterns, etc. ad inf. And we slogged through soft sand between creosote bushes over the dunes, skirting curlew tracks, to a marsh beside tidal estuaries (curving behind us) loaded with gulls, egrets, sandpipers.

and what's more
in shells of goose-like zombies
yet unborn—the speakers of the words
walk into a restaurant wholly of glass
a middle-aged woman comes to

1/6: On my desk are a green rock and a dead moth and ten stills from Peter Hutton films and a poorly calibrated postage scale. Looking "out" the window in front of me I see only the wall behind me. The author of *Discovering Moths* says, "Moths see lights that we do not." I've lived a week that you (dear reader) have not, and you've done the same—that is, you've not done the same.

emerging from sleep—
a middle-aged woman comes to
and "finishes" a sentence, producing a
     non-sequitur
as inappropriate as death and as terrifying
—it has absolutely no meaning

1/14: Columbine HS today, four sessions on haiku. Started eating in Boulder, finished south of Golden; good sandwich. Sun in my eyes, I couldn't find Pierce—then it hit me. Sign: "ordinary things" (white letters on red paper).

and it is
—it has absolutely no meaning
that is, it has absolutely no meaning
except as it becomes thicker and thicker
people stare, noticing how substantial

1/22: The day had an introduction, which it has no longer. Spent the first 2/3 of today working in the present prophetic tense, then as the sun set realized that the narrativist's past tense has the persuasive weight of a sack of sand. From fatuous seer to uncertain see-er—that's a brief account of my intellectual development today.

histories are, bodies—
people stare, noticing how substantial
the poodle: it dreams —but of what
and when? well!—now!: ça va sans
dire: the poodle's named Dire

1/27: Typed up pages and pages of
poems, acrostics of "**ECOLOGY**,"
both individually writ and of
passaround genesis, wrote a small
disquisition on it, went to Kinko's
prepping for Jenny complex class
handouts, washed dishes, napped,
listened to "2001" (mine), saw darkness
fall again. Incidentally, went to Kaiser's
and refused to pay $294 for inhalers …
things are tightening up.

creo que sí
dire: the poodle's named Dire
and he crashes mysteriously through
    Goethe's "Faust"
as my foot crashed through the roof
of the cozy Italian bar

2/14: Just a week ago I watched the
Missouri carrying small round cakes
of ice into the Mississippi,
some turning clockwise, others
counterclockwise for reasons S and
D and I couldn't figure out. We
speculated and, going further north,
looking up, we saw bald eagles swirling
in love or play over the monument
in Alton to the "martyr editor" Elijah
Lovejoy who was lynched in 1835 for
writing in his paper intransigently
against slavery.

from the dark
of the cozy Italian bar
I wake to the dark of experience
remembered—here is my body,
    here my
kaleidoscope: I see what's real

2/22: My right index finger got
infected ("staph") and swelled up
something awful. My regular doctor,
Anthony Leo, said it lacked "fluctuant
pus-y mass." I took it to Dr. Marti
Sharman, a very thin woman with
dyed black hair who cut it open,
drained it and has it recovering.
Purple, shredding skin, stuck in a
crook (which may stick). J bandages it
twice a day (plus her ingrown toenail).
We sit in the den to soak parts. Much
else is going on too.

as astonishment tableau
kaleidoscope: I see what's real
swallows up the above as a bushmaster
might swallow a cut diamond or a
cold wet circle a gold

2/26: Torrential rain fell Wednesday
morning. John Zorn and Ikue Mori
and Larry and I moved as a group
from one window to another, watching
the backyard fill with water from one,
watching the street in front rise over
the tires of cars from another. It was
only after the rain stopped that the
basement flooded. I've been working
on a sea saga that's going nowhere.

in the sun's
cold wet circle a gold
turning blue the bell at nine minutes
past the numb hour, the imperceptible
    present
—the ride we've somehow thumbed

3/5: Looking around for a topic, I see
of course (since I'm richly windowed
here) the huge snow that fell last
night, but I think, "Well, she wrote
about rain." Sudden thought: the word
"superfluous" is one of the loveliest
in the language. Right index finger's
slowly creeping back into the land of
the living. My version of the TV news
might begin, "As I speak to you in
this amazing fashion, a zillion tons of
particle-by-particle soil have slopped
their way into generalization."

made up of
—the ride we've somehow thumbed
per se plus its radiance etc. as
well as the mundane connotations:
    Clark Gable
(pretending he knows) knowing something

3/9: It is "officially" winter still, but
all the windows are open on this,
the warm, third springlike if not yet
spring evening of the year. The sound
of someone dragging a garbage can
seems at one moment to come from
the west, at the next from the north.
A single dog is barking all around.
The chickadees in the attic are quiet.

that's rarely considered
(pretending he knows) knowing something
—a preference for shadows over sun,
    circus,
decision—since no author but oneself
    has
decided what we are, feel

3/16: I heard that Dr. Marti had a
serious accident riding her bike and
being broadsided by a skateboarder.
Broken pelvis? Today at eleven J and
I go see Felice of Three Jewels,
income tax papers in hand. Wish
us luck! Wish us all luck.

like Shakespeare, who's
decided what we are, feel
and will become, period, but through a
social synapsis showing itself as attic
    window
once and future ancient Greek

4/1: We're using no euphemisms—it's "death" to the girls, not "sleep." At dying, spring has come to New England, a cold rain is falling through dull gray wind. The girls have twin umbrellas—developing characters, one and the other.

the questions that
once and future ancient Greek
articulations of reasoning interest
    posed to things
of the world as it appears, the
departure of those who survived

4/7: Friday, for KGNU's Pledge Drive, Sam Fuqua and I did a(nother) Yodeling Special, three hours of weird music, much of it obtained through Dutch scholar Bart Plantenga, all containing the universal yelp. We got a lot of calls—went over the top on a big "matching" pledge. Yahoo.

a little while
departure of those who survived
ramifying because nothing stays clumped
    together forever
even the sweetest grouping spreading
    itself out
and into the relative newness

4/12: New England now lies far to the East; northern California lies all around. There is something stranger than absence, and it is presence. I've been startled in and out of it (presence) over the course of the past four days. Is this a friend? Is this noon? Yes to the former, no the latter: it's 7:24 pm and the wind is blowing.

of continuing love
and into the relative newness
of love's breaking off—or branching,
    surely
(it's spring, after all, and nothing dies
entirely)—into shadow, dial, itch

4/18: Today Reed and I drove to the potholes near Greeley. Many ducks on Little Gaynor, flocks of ibis in farm fields, flashes of Swainson's hawks' underwing patterns, vast blackbird flocks, Virginia rail *kidick kidick* heard, but dried mud at our destination. Great blue herons copulating on rookery nest just west of Hygiene.

(to continue, not
entirely)—into shadow, dial, itch
—all of which means light, finger,
    rubbing
and their consolidation (minus the
    sense "solid")
into a purposeful act of

4/24: The late afternoon sun is still high in the sky and illuminating the "Joseph's Coat" roses along the back fence. Though I'm not disappointed that this is so, the yard is no farm. Anna and Martin's place is. We were there for five days, hauling feed, putting in seeds, taking delivery of a set of eleven 6-foot tall native trees.

understanding—a glimpse
into a purposeful act of
caring, I mean, producing circumstantial
    meaning of
our own, shared making, broadly
    shared that
is with typists, toads, consequence

5/3: Five days in Idalia, almost on the Kansas line, population 80 but the school has 150 kids (farm families). They've won prizes for bringing in special programs by holding repeated cookiedough sales. Community shines more strongly as commercial American "culture" thins. The extreme flatness, there, is thrilling, and I realized too that treelessness (though trees are so dear) releases an excitement into the air.

—that's how it
is with typists, toads, consequences
you can't quite put your finger on
which element will squirt and which will
dissipate into unmarked layers of

5/10: Some days sustain mostly mental events, others are more constantly physical. My new relationship (with Moreña) is both (though mostly mental today, since she's far away). The thought (or concept) of "farm families" in these times raises images of soldiers, mere kids being cynically maneuvered into battles that should never have happened. Moreña is steering clear.

data—pretty things
dissipate into unmarked layers of
consciously perceived or maybe only
    half-glimpsed neither
auspicious nor ominous events which
    return to
memory unearthed and aired—sung

Shims

SHIMS

Blatant
pattern through
shrinking and expanding
unfinished tapestries, show yourself!

―――

A child's inbound anxieties
roll together like
outbound hostilities
aerodynamically

―――

Soup?
for two
or even four
stands hot in bowls

―――

Everything false falls away
as Earth's crust
shakes ferns
(yo-di-láy-ee!)

―――

Quick
as rivals
neutrality and light
improve hindsight, disprove prophecy

―――

Somewhere east of Java
suggesting it's suggestive
western sounds
subtitle

In the thick of
standing wave clouds
political thought
condenses

―――

Kindergarten
implies weeding
W and X-ylophoning
which wind up WAX

―――

Elmer's "yellow streak" showed
in milky glue
no matter
free

―――

Freud
looked in
trepidation into her
dream of dandelion fluff

―――

Preoccupied by big themes
the mother bear
sniffs air,
hesitates

―――

Ditty-mongering
growl Hopis
there're mourning loops
Second Mesa pure yellow

When
suddenness's becalmed
some snakes assume
coils—spring's attentive étude

———

But close-dancing is so
perpendicular to desire,
my dear
wind

———

Warren
winding, porous
but scarcely harmless
harbors our inexcusable habits

———

In Albuquerque she found
the vertical sun
everywhere, even
gradual

———

Iodine
forted animal
in neglected sandstone
works the minimal unbrokenly

———

Orange edges around stark
widening winter-wizened projections
with sexy
fringes

———

Sometimes
bunking explanation

Utopian gravel's spreading out
woodchuck light condenses
sour chalk
bingo

———

Credulity
settles it
—skepticism under silt
crumbles just like that

———

Remotely a blur (mirage,
then not) become
an impediment
hit

———

Ill-sorted
lawyers lay
bastion beside brevity,
emerged with pure basalt

———

Crescent oxen given walk
arrive with milk
from manuscripts
(metaphorically)

———

Impassioned
fast brown
greens up querulously
forming a dense bed

———

How funnily illogicality medicates
Muybridge's dactylic approaches

lies in toto
naked as a tongue

——

Once upon a time
catch us mid-reconnoiter
the sun
webbed

——

First
under leaves
der Maulwurf, second
sun below horizon, third

——

It was a dark
and now's bright
as pitch
cliff

——

Split
half-dollar spent
on purple milk
suited to our situation

——

They thought of it
solitary alternative board
notwithstanding, it
showed

——

Tubeworms
without prelude
circled the line
set in pavement photography

painlessly astride
billions

——

Portability
gets complicated
thoughts riled up
three times as much

——

Hallucinations of a bell
ringer include procreation
and funeral
appetizers

——

Twelve-toned
slices notes
the Viennese conductor
clears his throat / again

——

And immediately pigeons descend
Nell merely records
humbling winds'
origins

——

Porridge
being sucked
as armies draw
mutual portraits in charcoal

——

Shostakovich resounds like mine
tailings shaken in
owl flight
now

"Amethysts? No." Tim said,
"the building's calm,
full of
clack"

———

Count
seven cows
back to front
hunkering synonymous with home

———

My logic dictates that
and chance this,
which is
blooming

———

You
and another
you surround me
with too much difference

Drawn
up awkwardly
toward unsought choice
her life nevertheless gleamed

———

Silent and tall alphabet
front to back
zipping aft
discordantly

———

Slanted
algebra fills
the filigreed fate
and Tycho Brahe smiles

———

Two aphorisms never meet
because structure intervenes
—truth's contradictory
hedge

Postface

In 1992, having met at the Naropa Summer Writing Program (to which Lyn had been invited as a guest writer/teacher for a week), we began composing poems collaboratively. We opted to communicate by "snail-mail" rather than utilize a faster technology, in part because Jack was not (and is not) a computer user, but also so as to preserve the unhurried pace of the more traditional, contemplative epistolary space.

Beginning with the exchange of free-verse lines that (some 300 mailings later) became *Sunflower* (originally published by The Figures in 2000), we gradually multiplied and diversified our projects. Soon, a typical exchange would include ten or so formally different works.

Only one of these works, called "Interview," is not included in this volume; we anticipate that it will appear as an independent book, a companion (though not a necessary companion) to this one.

Apart from "Interview," all the poems we've composed together to date are collected here. There are eleven of them.

"Questionably" is subject only to one rule: it is composed entirely of questions. It lacks narrative coherence, but, as we came to realize, it builds an affective structure—nervous, melancholy, hilarious, and, of course, inquisitive. At heart, "Questionably" celebrates curiosity—or rather (since all our collaborations have been motivated by curiosity) it does so explicitly. We are both, it should be said, enthusiasts of the kinds of investigations that pre-technological natural historians undertook, largely, if not simply, out of curiosity.

"Revival" carries on the very loose, even casual, form of "Sunflower," unfolding without any other goal than that of discovering (or generating) the surprises contingent on unfolding itself.

"Paddle" is a sentence-based (rather than lineated) work, built of non-sequiturs.

"Wicker" and "Crisscross" are formally related. Both are 2-part works, laid out in columns, and in both the right hand, five-line stanzas adhere to a rather strict, pre-determined form, invented by Lyn and Jack but inspired by the Japanese renga. Each line of each stanza contains a set number of words, 2, 3, 4, 5, 3 for "Wicker" and 3, 5, 7, 7, 5 for "Crisscross." In both poems, the last line of each stanza is repeated as the second line of the next—setting up an interlinkage that is intentionally tricky. Every stanza swings on a hinge—but waiting to see what the other will bring forth when she or he opens the gate was part of the pleasure.

The material in the left hand column of "Wicker" consists of quotations from famous, unknown, or purely imaginary, people. Many of the quotations are correctly attributed; some are not. The material in the left hand column of "Crisscross" consists of journal entries—according to the rule we imposed on ourselves, they had to refer to something that had "really happened."

The eight poems of the sequence that comprises "The Abecedarian's Dream" adhere to three rules: the poems are alphabetical acrostics, each line contains 10 words, and every fourth line rhymes—somehow, somewhere.

"On Laughter" is a play—a Punch and Judy melodrama—whacking humor over the head. The play casts one of us in the A role, the other in as B; we could each "speak" for as long or as short as we wanted, as long as we spoke of laughter (or provoked it). The only elements that were set were the dialogic form and the theme—laughter in any of its manifestations.

The lines of "Horizon," like those of "Sunflower" and "Revival," were allowed to flow without predetermined limits, but the poems that comprise the series adhere to an acrostic element, and that gives them a potentially proverbial trajectory, at least in outline.

"Blanks" utilizes something of a Mad-Libs structure. As usual, we took turns adding to the work, in this case by reaching into each other's entries: each addition included three blanks in its text; the respondent had to fill in the blanks and then provide additional text. The piece acquired its own haphazard logic.

The pyramid and reverse-pyramid form of "Shims" is self-evident. The two columns were in composition simultaneously, accordioning an unpredictable melody.

We've tried not to try hard with the various shapes, rules, suggestions, and restrictions, but to let the works have (and show) their own topologies. Form can be simple geometry, we find, and set up "trigonometric" growths and more.

We tried for that—and, of course, for each other.

We both feel that our individual writings have been much enriched by the fun and special impulses of these tradeoffs. We've each learned deepenings of the act of choice.